FAERY CRAFT

About the Author

Emily Carding (Cornwall, United Kingdom) is an author, artist, and priestess. An initiate of Alexandrian Wicca and a member of the Starstone Network, Carding has been working with inner world Faery contacts since childhood. She has been trained in techniques of Celtic shamanism by John and Caitlín Matthews, and has worked with renowned Faery teachers R. J. Stewart and Brian and Wendy Froud. A respected and active member of the Faery and tarot community, Carding's work has received international recognition.

Visit her online at ChildOfAvalon.com.

Emily Carding

FAERY CRAFT

Weaving Connections with the Enchanted Realm

Llewellyn Publications
Woodbury, Minnesota

FIRST EDITION
Fourth Printing, 2016

Book design and edit by Rebecca Zins
Cover and color page design by Lisa Novak
Cover images: grunge weathered circular: iStockphoto.com/Roy Konitzer,
grunge spring frame: iStockphoto.com/Megan Tamaccio, grunge swirls
background: iStockphoto.com/Aleksandar Velasevic, grunge corners,
Arabesque decoration, textured background: iStockphoto.com/David Crooks
Interior photos and illustrations are credited by individual pieces;
floral and Celtic ornaments are from Dover Publications

Llewellyn Publications is a registered trademark of Llewellyn Worldwide Ltd.

Library of Congress Cataloging-in-Publication Data
Carding, Emily.
Faery craft : weaving connections with the enchanted realm / Emily Carding.—1st ed.
    p. cm.
Includes bibliographical references and index.
ISBN 978-0-7387-3133-9
1. Fairies. I. Title.
BF1552.C37 2012
133.9—dc23

                                                    2012022818

Llewellyn Worldwide Ltd. does not participate in, endorse, or have any authority or responsibility concerning private business transactions between our authors and the public.
    All mail addressed to the author is forwarded, but the publisher cannot, unless specifically instructed by the author, give out an address or phone number.
    Any Internet references contained in this work are current at publication time, but the publisher cannot guarantee that a specific location will continue to be maintained. Please refer to the publisher's website for links to authors' websites and other sources.

Llewellyn Publications
A Division of Llewellyn Worldwide Ltd.
2143 Wooddale Drive
Woodbury, MN 55125-2989
www.llewellyn.com

Printed in the United States of America

This book is dedicated to that Faery being
who is reading over your left shoulder right now…

Contents

The Faery Prince

A Faery Prince has snared my heart

Hiding it deep within his own

From all things mortal kept apart

Where roots and brambles overgrown

Guard it well against the light

And keep it green and shadowed there

Though I have searched by starry night

And in the spring sun warm and fair

Not prince nor heart may yet be found

But promised whispers on the breeze

And sweetest music in the ground

Lead my senses with their tease

So I must venture in between

Where dusky rose sings her lament

And seek by twilight what lies unseen

With hope to heal what has been rent…

Emily Carding, 2011

Preface

I was honoured when I was asked by Llewellyn to write a book about Faery lifestyle and practices, but I was also daunted. How could I convey to others a connection and way of life that has always been so instinctive and natural to me?

As a child I would go on missions for the faeries in my dreams, passing through a little wooden door in a hill and visiting a magnificent underworld realm of vivid colours and magickal creatures both menacing and benign. It was not until much later in life that I would learn of the truth behind these visions and the legacy of the Faery tradition, in which the Faery beings dwelt in the hollow hills. How fascinated I was to learn that my dreams had revealed this realm to me! The diminutive flower fairies of English lore had never held the same kind of wonder.

My connection with this realm led to an aura of otherworldliness that made many people uncomfortable, including my parents, when I would spend the longest time simply contemplating a blade of grass in the garden, admiring its microcosmic magnitude!

Upon leaving home for university, I was soon able to develop my fascination for magick and the otherworld with the discovery of a local magickal community. As my college was within the grounds of a nature reserve, most of my time was spent by the lake in the company of trees rather than in class, but it was there where I learnt the lessons of most value.

My connection with the Faery realm has strengthened still more over the years, and I have felt their presence with me through life's many ups and downs. Divorce and motherhood set me on a completely new path, one I never could have planned for, as it has seen me leave my work in theatre for a new career as an artist and author, creating work with the aid of my guides and allies that opens gateways to the otherworld. This includes the groundbreaking *Transparent Tarot* (Schiffer Books, 2008) and its sister deck *The Transparent Oracle* (Schiffer Books, 2010), which brings together aspects of shamanism, Faery lore, and ceremonial magick in an original structure based on the seven directions. Though published more recently, my first creation of this kind was *The Tarot of the Sidhe* (Schiffer Books, 2011), a series of seventy-eight visionary paintings created over a year and a day using methods of trance channelling.

Over the last few years, I have discovered and immersed myself in the vibrant Faery community through festivals and events. Upon first glance it can seem flaky and superficial, but there is so much love and genuine magick to be found within! A large section of this book is dedicated to the beautiful, creative, and inspirational people of this community.

At the same time, I am equally involved in the magickal community as an initiate of Alexandrian Wicca and member of the Starstone Network, a network of Wiccan covens and groves founded by Sorita D'Este and David Rankine. I have a keen interest in varied aspects of magickal practice, including Qabalah and Western Mystery tradition, and have trained in Celtic shamanic techniques with renowned teachers Caitlín and John Matthews. I am also a torchbearer in the Covenant of Hekate.

I have pieced together the advice and exercises within this book through analysing my own experiences and with the guidance of my own inner contacts. My goal is to help the reader, with time and patience, to create and strengthen a connection to nature and her hidden inhabitants. I have attempted to consciously re-create those simple yet powerful moments in which connection and magick may be found. Alongside these lifestyle building blocks, if you will, is as much information about the different paths and various ways people have of expressing their love and commitment to Faery as I could possibly fit into one book, so that you may find what inspires you. May it be a torch to light your way.

This book can be what you want or need it to be. The simply curious may just read through it to catch a glimpse of the lives of others. Those who are truly called to work with Faery and wish to deepen their connection may find within the contents of these pages a labyrinthine map with many routes. It is not my intention to spoon-feed—rather, I prefer to open the door to an adventure. It is your choice to pass through; indeed, which path will you take? Follow your heart, and your own true path to the hidden realms will reveal itself to you…

Introduction

The world of Faery has always been with us—from the time of our ancient ancestors and their deep connection with the land, forged from the need to survive; through the rise of Christianity, merging new beliefs with the old ways; through the Industrial Revolution and humankind's rising need to "tame" nature; all the way into the twenty-first century. Beliefs and practices have changed much over the centuries, as fluid and mercurial as the shapeshifting realm of the otherworld itself, and yet, through all of that, the core of truth remains.

One hundred years ago, the anthropologist Walter Evans-Wentz undertook a remarkable task. Over the course of many months, he travelled to a great number of locations within the Celtic landscape of Scotland, Ireland, Wales, Brittany, the Isle of Man, and Cornwall and interviewed those who had personal tales to tell of contact with the Faery realm or valuable gems of folklore. Most of the eyewitnesses he managed to interview for *The Faery-Faith in Celtic Countries* were extremely elderly, and it must have seemed as though contact with Faery was a fading relic of the past, a victim of the rising tide of industry and technology. Yet here and now, in an era of rapid progress and almost unbelievable technology, it is clear that the Faery faith is not only alive and well but thriving. After all, here you are—reading this book!

Why Faery Craft, not Faery Faith?

For good or bad, we do not live in an age of faith; we live in an age of science and proven results. However, there is no need to see this as being in opposition to a practice of magick or interaction with otherworldly beings. On the contrary, the need for experiential evidence and transformative results from our actions and interactions can do nothing but strengthen what is true and enable us to discard what is false or ineffective. These results may be subtle indeed, but for those who make genuine contact with the Faery realm, life will not be the same again.

Of course, this is also an age of quick fixes and instant gratification, which is a path that benefits no one. In order to truly gain wisdom and evolve as spiritual beings, we need the discipline of "Craft." The term *Faery faith* implies a passive, though respectful, belief passed down through generations without it necessarily involving any experimentation, effort, or discovery. Faery Craft, on the other hand, is more evocative of a practical approach of work and collaboration with the Faery realm. The Craft is, of course, also a well-known term for Wicca and Witchcraft, for much the same reason: it is a discipline that requires practice and skill and produces results. So are you ready to roll up your sleeves?

Of course, it's not all work and no play—this is Faery we're talking about, after all! The Craft is, in essence, referring to the art of integrating Faery into our day-to-day lives, not as a form of escapism but as a way of truly engaging with the world on a deeper level.

A Note on the Spelling

For those of you drawn to this subject for the first time, the spelling of Faery/faerie as opposed to the usual "fairy" is used to differentiate between the modern, disempowered fantasy creation and the authentic living beings (faeries) and tradition (Faery), which can be surprisingly different from expectations!

Before We Go Any Further, What Exactly Is Faery?

*"Something from the dawn of time. Who
could possibly put a name to that?"*

Captain Jack Harkness in "Small Worlds" (*Torchwood* season one)

• • • • • • •

There is certainly no "exactly" when it comes to Faery! What we understand as the Faery realm today is an umbrella term that covers a huge variety of beings and phenomena, from the piskies of Cornwall to the tall and noble sidhe of the Gaelic lands. But the Faery realm is by no means solely Celtic in nature or tradition. It encompasses the spirits of place and nature and otherworldly beings of the entire globe, which can vary in size and appearance as much as the landscape of the world itself—from the small yet potent to beings of almost unfathomable size.

They are the intelligence behind the living force of the planet, and as such they reflect the wondrous variety of our vibrant world. Their nature may be highly individual, part of a mass consciousness, or anywhere between, but they are living beings—with their own existences, functions, and goals—who inhabit a realm that is only separated from our own through a difference in frequency or resonance. Essentially they are around us all the time, in a more fluid and intangible form than our own comparatively solid reality. This makes sense on a scientific level when you realize that all matter is essentially energy, and its solidity is solely dependent on the speed at which the atoms are vibrating.

*"Can you wonder that the People of the Hills don't care
to be confused with that painty-winged, wand-waving,
sugar-and-shake-your-head set of impostors?"*

Rudyard Kipling, *Puck of Pook's Hill*

• • • • • • •

We can add to our understanding by taking a moment to look at what they are not, for there are many misconceptions lurking in the guise of certain New Age teachings. They are not reflections of aspects of our personality, though they may choose to reflect those to us at times. Reducing magick and the otherworld to psychology is, in my opinion, one of the most harmful developments in magickal practice of the modern age. Neither are they all tiny winged striped-socks-wearing beings, though they may appear that way if they so choose. This is simply a modern fashion overhaul of the Victorian flower fairy. Faery beings do not simply giggle and play all day, though many are indeed fun loving, but they are as much a balance of light and dark as we are ourselves. I would also like to emphasize that working with them is about achieving mutual goals, not self-help. They do not exist purely to enhance our lives, though of course our lives are indeed greatly enhanced by their presence.

What is crucial to understanding is that Faery beings are our close relatives in the spiritual realm (hence they were and still are often referred to as "cousins"), and we are already connected to them, whether we are aware of it or not. The door is open—we need merely to learn how to perceive it and have the courage and discipline to walk through…

Why Work with Faery?

We are incomplete without interaction with the invisible realms of the inner earth. The land that Faery beings inhabit is the vibrant inner landscape of our world, where the full potency of the primal powers are preserved and may be accessed through our work to revitalize our own land and its inhabitants. To walk the earth in the pretence that all that exists is what is on the surface is almost like living off the leaves of a carrot. We may get dirt under our fingernails, but to delve a little deeper brings great rewards!

Denial of the spirit within the land has brought with it such severe destruction that the lasting consequences cannot be known. Although this century brings with it many great wonders, it also brings new terrors. Although we cannot know in detail the spiritual practices of our ancient ancestors, who depended on the land for their survival, in many ways we find ourselves full circle. We cannot help but be aware of the environmental crisis we find ourselves approaching, and our true dependence on the powers of nature is becoming more and more clear. Humankind's attempt to tame the wild earth is failing, so it is time to revive our connection with the land through communion with our Faery allies. It is a common tendency to reach out to magickal beings for help, as we see them as being capable of great wonders beyond our means. However, it is of key importance to understand that in order to be truly effective in the physical realm, there are certain things that they need our help with. When we work with Faery, the whole definitely becomes more than the sum of its parts.

How Can This Book Help?

Faery Craft brings together many strands of practice like never before to give you a comprehensive guide to human-faery relations. Together we will look not only at ancient folklore but also at contemporary experiences in the context of relevance to our own work with Faery, and we will explore practical exercises to expand our awareness and form new bonds with the spirits of the land. We will also be deepening our connection and perception of the elemental beings of earth, air, fire, and water as part of our awareness of the world around us. We will learn how to create sacred space, how to use tools from the world of nature, and how to recognize and locate places of power within the landscape.

There are many ways to work with Faery, and though it can be an individual path, we will also take an objective look at some of the traditions and teachings that have developed over the years and see what they may have to offer. Join me while we take an inside look at how different individuals and groups working (and playing!) in the world today express their connection and love for Faery, including the modern phenomenon of the Faery festival. We will explore the creative expression of the Faery community through interviews with some of the most outstanding artists, musicians, and authors in the field.

How to Use This Book

Faery Craft consists of eight chapters, each of which is designed to build your strengths in the different qualities needed for Faery contact. The structure is built around the symbol of the Faery Star, or septagram, a symbol which has been used with many varying meanings throughout history and which I have used here in *Faery Craft* with original interpretations and meanings inspired by my own work with Faery. The "Faery Craft septagram" (as I have dubbed it) connects each point of the star with the seven directions of north, south, east, west, above, below, and within, which in turn are connected with the four elements and the sun, moon, and stars. From these we find our key qualities needed

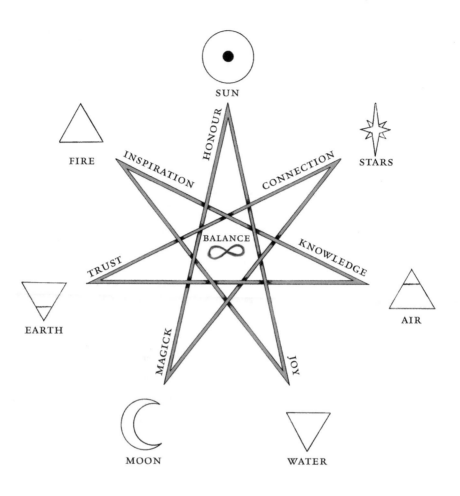

SUN

HONOUR

FIRE

INSPIRATION

CONNECTION

STARS

TRUST

BALANCE
∞

KNOWLEDGE

EARTH

MAGICK

JOY

AIR

MOON

WATER

Faery Craft septagram
by Tamara Newman
(www.tamaranewman.com)

within ourselves for Faery Craft: knowledge from the east and the corresponding element of air (chapter 1), connection from the stars and the direction above (chapter 2), trust from earth in the north (chapter 3), honour from the direction of within and the power of the sun (chapter 4), magick from the moon and the direction of below (chapter 5), joy from the west and the element of water (chapter 6), and inspiration from the element of fire in the south (chapter 7).

The eighth chapter represents the central point of balance within the star, where all the qualities meet. This may seem complicated or confusing now, especially if you are unfamiliar with the directions and elements, but don't worry—all will become clear as the book progresses.

Seven Months in Faery

There is a tradition within Faery lore that tells of people taken into Faery for periods of seven months or seven years. If you feel drawn to do so, you may choose to take a chapter a month and work through the exercises contained within and at the end of each chapter a number of times during that month. This will give you time to thoroughly explore each quality and pace yourself as you progress, enabling you to establish practices and routines that will enrich your relationship with the world and its hidden depths for the rest of your life. Faery Craft cannot be rushed. There are exercises contained within each chapter and also additional exercises and suggested activities at the end of each chapter in order to make it clear to follow.

I strongly suggest that you keep a notebook or journal in order to record your experiences and progress, including any interesting dreams you may have during this time. Faery experiences can be powerful, but they can also be subtle, and it will be easier to remember key moments, messages, and images if you keep a good record. Things that may seem insignificant or nonsensical at the time can gain meaning later on.

Take my hand as I lead you through the pages of this book. Let us adventure together, discovering our own unique gifts and strengths that we can bring to the world of Faery, working together with our Faery cousins to build bridges between our worlds so that we need no longer dwell in the damaging and painful illusion of disconnection.

CHAPTER ONE
Knowledge

We begin our journey into Faery in the direction of east, the element of air, and the quality of knowledge. Within the Western Mystery tradition, which has been highly influential in most modern esoteric teachings, the element of air is associated with logic, law, and the mental realm. This led clearly to my choice of knowledge as being the quality to be associated with this direction and element.

In order to be able to better understand your experiences as you progress through the book, it is essential to have some background knowledge on the subject. This will mean that you are building on a strong foundation, enabling you to place any experiences into context and equipping you with the necessary tools of interpretation and discrimination. It also helps prevent making easy yet critical mistakes due to simply not knowing any better! If early time is spent in dedication to learning as much as possible about Faery lore and history, as well as the traditions of the land around you, then this knowledge has time to properly grow within you like a seed, as you nourish it with the spiritual work of the successive chapters.

In this chapter we will cover the origins and nature of Faery, the concept of hierarchy, the darker side of Faery, basic etiquette, Faery beasts, and important symbols that are connected with the Faery realm.

The Origins and Nature of Faery

*"When the first baby laughed for the first time, its laugh
broke into a thousand pieces, and they all went skipping
about, and that was the beginning of fairies. And now
when every new baby is born, its first laugh becomes a
fairy. So there ought to be one fairy for every boy or girl."*

J. M. Barrie, Peter Pan and Wendy

· · · · · · ·

Unlike the fairies of J. M. Barrie's Neverland, we do not need to believe in Faery beings
in order for them to exist, any more than we need to believe in the postman to receive
our mail. But even those of us with close connections to the elusive Faery realm can find
it difficult to explain exactly who they are, for their origins are as mysterious as their
destiny, which is inextricably tied to our own.

As definitions and understandings grow and change over the years, the term Faery
has come to cover a vast variety of beings. In many ways, the more you learn, the more
confusing it becomes, as the lines between faeries, gods, angels, elementals, ghosts, and
other spirits become very blurred, if indeed those lines exist at all in some cases. We can
expand our understanding by looking at myth and folklore. It is then up to individuals
to find, through their own experiential and intellectual exploration, their own insights,
the grain of original truth that formed the pearl of myth.

Nature Spirits

*"They were not the same as nature spirits, though they
were allied to them. They were a race apart, with their own
laws and rulers, their own ambitions and occupations,
marriages, births and even, at long last, deaths."*

Christina Hole, English Folklore

· · · · · · ·

As explained in the introduction, the term Faery has become, in recent years, an
umbrella term for many different classes of beings, though they were more distinctly
divided in the past. This, allied with the wide availability of works founded on fancy
rather than experience or research, may lead to some confusion. The modern interpreta-

tion of Faery beings is that they are first and foremost nature spirits—that is, the spirits of trees, plants, rivers, and the spirits of place. Perhaps that is because it is these beings who most call out for our attention at this time of environmental crisis, and forming a connection with these beings certainly forms the basis of most Faery work, as indeed it does in this book.

However, if you look into older teachings and folklore, which are the only real written sources we have at our disposal, we can see that there is a distinct race, or perhaps several races, of beings whose existence is clearly connected to, yet independent of, the land. Activities such as stealing babies and kidnapping midwives to look after them, or even stealing away young women for breeding purposes, speak of a dwindling race living out of time, who have, in the past, mixed their blood with ours to keep them from extinction. Are such stories simply propaganda on the part of a church wishing to keep the powers of the otherworld as something to be feared? It becomes very difficult to know for certain. The Faery race (or races) was always considered to be made up of powerful beings who were often to be feared, especially if crossed in any way. Throughout the old tales it is clear that they have lives and a culture that is distinct and comparable with our own, with marriages, births, and funerals. Though it has been suggested that these may be simple mockeries or reflections of our civilization, there seems to be more depth to it than that—some subtle and intrinsic connection with our own lives and events. Through my own otherworldly contacts, I have experienced events that reflect our own customs, but with a very distinct cultural identity of their own. Thus it may be inaccurate terminology to refer to the Faery race as nature spirits, yet they are inhabitants and guardians of the inner landscape of our world, just as we are of the outer landscape, no matter what poor a job we make of our guardianship.

Nature spirits are an extremely important part of Faery work. We may see them as a point of mutual interaction and responsibility between ourselves and the Faery race—and, through them, the world soul, a relationship in which we are currently out of balance. Nature spirits may be found in all traditions around the world, reflecting the nature of the varying landscapes that they inhabit. In the Hindu tradition they are known as Vidyeshvaras, the guardians of the living world. In ancient Greece the legends are full of nymphs, dryads, and satyrs, who often mix and interbreed both with humans

Julia Jeffrey, "Queen of the Skies"

and gods. Native cultures around the world have a close relationship with the spirits of their land and a deep awareness of the mutual need for that connection.

It is worth noting that the wilder and more inhospitable to human life the landscape is, the stronger and potentially more dangerous the spirits of that place will be. Hence in mountainous regions you will find great tall beings and races of giants, but in mostly domesticated and inhabited areas, the nature spirits can seem much gentler and smaller, unless there is an underlying power to the place that remains.

Even when experienced in connecting with the spirits of the land, it can take some adjustment when travelling—normally a few days spent in an unfamiliar or ancestrally alien landscape—to make the energetic shift necessary to perceive them, but they are always there. To connect with the living energies of the world around us, from the tiniest flower to the greatest continent, is to live in harmony with our Faery cousins and experience a deeper understanding of the world and its needs. Since the realm of Faery is so all-encompassing and fluid in its nature, it is difficult and confusing to dwell too much on terminology, but it is beneficial to reach the understanding that not all beings that we think of as being Faery have the same natures, powers, or origins. As with any experience of Faery, if we try to grasp it too tightly, our understanding may slip away. Certainly the closer you look, the more blurred any dividing lines become between faeries, nature spirits, elementals, spirits of place, and even the ancient gods.

Ancient Gods

"The earlier Celtic Gods and Goddesses are better represented among the fairies. Morgan le Fay is generally considered to descend from Morrigan, the War Goddess. Aynia, who is the Fairy Queen in Tyrone, is one form of Anu…"

Katharine Briggs, *The Fairies in Tradition and Literature*

. . . .

For anyone used to the modern-day disempowered image of the tiny, childlike, winged fairy that lives in a mushroom or shyly hides behind a flower, it would seem quite a leap to suggest that many Faery beings were, or indeed are, gods. However, you do not need to delve very deeply into ancient tradition to discover that most of what are considered to be Faery kings and queens have also been worshipped as gods, nor indeed do you need to take many steps into their world to understand the power that they hold.

One of the best-known examples of a crossover between deities and Faery lore may be found in the ancient Celtic myths of the Tuatha de Danann, our best source for which is the famous Book of Invasions. Though the text dates back to the eleventh century, the original sources are widely believed to date back much further, incorporating material from as far back as the fourth century CE.

Through the ancient myths, we learn that the Tuatha de Danann (children of Danu) were a powerful race of magickal beings who inhabited Ireland before they were driven underground by the Milesians, a race of mortal men. They arrived on ships from the four mystical cities of Falias, Gorias, Murias, and Finias, bringing with them treasures that bear a remarkable resemblance to the four grail hallows of Arthurian lore: the spear of Lugh, the sword of Nuada, the stone of Fal, and the cauldron of the Dagda; we can also recognize these treasures in the four suits of the tarot. The Tuatha de Danann are considered to be the pre-Christian gods of Ireland; interestingly, they were preceded by a race of giants called the Firbolgs, with whom they shared the land for a while before eventually going to war with another race of giants, the Fomorians. Both may be compared to the Titans of Greek mythology, great primal forces of the planet who were overcome eventually by the Olympian pantheon we are familiar with today. Indeed, there are many tales throughout the world of an ancient race of giants who inhabited the earth before humanity, and these are also significant in Faery lore. The sidhe (pronounced *shee*), the Faery people of the Celtic lands, are believed to be the descendants of these gods and, in some cases, the gods themselves.

Probably the best-known example of one of the sidhe who is both a Faery queen and a goddess is the Irish war goddess named the Morrigan. She plays a major part in all the battles of the Tuatha de Danann and is a significant power within the Celtic pantheon. Her name has been given to many places within the Celtic landscape, and her influence can be seen to spread through the lands and ages into many other tales and cultures. True to her shapeshifting nature, she has many guises, most notably Morgan le Fay of the Arthurian tales. Other people of the sidhe who may be considered deities include Lugh, a solar deity from whom we get the Irish harvest festival of Lughnasadh; Nuada of the silver hand, who was their king; Manannan Mac Lir, a god of the sea; and Etain, who was both a sorceress and a goddess of sovereignty.

Scotland brings us strong, powerful giantess faery queens to suit its rugged landscape and unforgiving climate. Here we find such fascinating figures as the Cailleach, a great shapeshifter of tremendous strength who is often credited with forming the landscape, whose presence may be seen in folklore throughout the British Isles and beyond. A similar figure may be found in Nicneven, the great faery queen of Scottish lore who dwells beneath the mountain Ben Nevis. She has often been equated with the ancient Greek goddess Hekate, seen as being not only the queen of the Faeries, but also of witches and the dead.

Nearby Wales also gives us a rich vein of Faery gods and goddesses, including Gwyn Ap Nudd, the king of the Tylwyth Teg (the Welsh Faery race), who rules the Welsh underworld, Annwn, and leads the wild hunt with his Faery hounds.

In other lands, similarly blurred lines may be found between Faery and deity. Within Nordic tradition we find gods such as Loki, who is descended from giants (who again are defeated by the Nordic pantheon), and Freyr, who is the king of Alfheim, the land of the light elves. In fact, the Nordic gods are separated into two races, the Aesir and the Vanir, and the Vanir share many qualities with Faery races such as the sidhe, such as great beauty and the gifts of prophecy and sorcery. They are also deeply connected to agriculture and the land. In his book *Leechcraft*, Stephen Pollington tells us that while "the Norse myths mostly concern the two main races of gods—Aesir and Vanir—the poetic tradition often juxtaposes Aesir and Alvar as 'gods and elves.'"

The name Freyr, or Frey, translates as "lord," and the name of his twin sister of the Vanir, Freya, translates as "lady," but it is unclear whether there is any connection to the title sometimes given to the trooping faeries of lords and ladies or, indeed, the titles of the Wiccan God and Goddess, who are often referred to as Lord and Lady; it would appear to be no more than a curious coincidence. However, Freya also has some definite parallels with Faery, being the psychopomp queen of the Valkyries, who, with their connection to battle and the dead, as well as an association with ravens, display some strong connections to the Irish Morrigan.

Freyr is sometimes referred to as a horned god, and like horned gods of other traditions, he is strongly associated with fertility, both of humans and the land itself. Indeed, most deities that are considered to be kings of Faery are depicted as horned and have this same association with fertility. Like Pan of Greek mythology, many display a voracious

Professor Ari Berk on Faeries and the Dead

WE WOULD MUCH prefer to see tiny fairies in floral dresses and so on, but the truth behind this idea of fairies as little children is part of an older, dark tradition that people are really not too excited to hear about. When you start talking about Faery lore and the disposition of the souls of unbaptised children, a lot of people are ready to turn off. That's it—back to the Disney Channel! But really this is where so much of the lore originates: in loss, in mourning, in wanting to know the dead remain close to us, in our desire to continue our conversations with those we love. In this branch of lore, Faerieland becomes a kind of earthly limbo. But this is only one aspect of Faery.

If you ask me what a Faery is, it's impossible to answer in one breath. It's a word that has so many meanings and many incarnations. Is a faery the house Lar of the ancient Roman household? That's one version, one mask, and a very old one that still has resonance. Is a faery a spirit of the dead? Yes, absolutely. That is one area of Faery lore that is much ignored now, in favour of a fluffier kind of faery. That's because we don't like obligation, as a society. Faery lore is filled with obligation. You are resident in this place or that place, and many, many successive generations of people have lived there before you. What is your obligation to these people who are most likely nameless? From their earliest appearances in story and lore, faeries have represented the nameless dead of the land. We have lineage ancestors whom we know, but then there are the—may I call them "landcestors"? These are the oldest spirits of place whose names are often forgotten but who still must be acknowledged. Sometimes these come to us as faeries.

Faeries as the ancient dead should be really relevant to us, because most of us do not live in the same town or village where we were born, so lore that tries to bridge the gap between newcomers and the local landcestors (it's an official word now), the past residents of a place, is vitally important. We tend to look forward only, and that means we lose our sense of obligation to a place. That means at a town council meeting, we're more likely to vote to put the new parking lot over the ancient burial mound, because we've forgotten or refuse to learn the stories of the places where we choose to reside…

Faery lore is about interdimensional respect—respect between people and their past. It helps to not think about yourself purely as yourself. Our edges appear to be finite, but they're not; we're interconnected in a thousand ways with our environment, but we forget that so easily! This kind of lore helps one to reestablish those links.

Ari Berk in an interview with the author in 2011. Ari Berk is a world-renowned expert on folklore and mythology, with a large number of published titles to his name, including *The Runes of Elfland* (with artist Brian Froud), *The Secret History of Giants*, and *Coyote Speaks: Wonders of the Native American World* (with Carolyn Dunn). He is also an accomplished writer of fiction and is the author of *Death Watch* (book one of The Undertaken Trilogy). Dr. Berk is Professor of English at Central Michigan University, teaching courses in mythology, folklore, American Indian studies, and medieval literature. He is also the former editor of the *Realms of Fantasy* magazine's Folkroots section and sits on the board of directors of the Mythic Imagination Institute. His work can be explored via his website at www.ariberk.com.

sexual appetite and priapic qualities, which are normally combined with a lack of morality as we would understand it; so, ladies, be warned! These are real and very powerful energies.

Other horned gods who are considered kings of Faery include Cernunnos of Celtic tradition, Herne the Hunter of English folklore, and Gwyn ap Nudd and his earlier counterpart Arawn of Welsh mythology. Veles, or Volos, of the Slavic culture is another horned god who, though not overtly linked to the Faery lore of that land, is seen as ruler of the underworld and the dead. Similarly, the ram-horned god of ancient Egypt, Khnum, was associated with fertility and the underworld. This chthonic role is strongly associated with Faery, as both the ancestors and the Faery race may be found in the underworld.

When we look at deities who are considered to be Faery queens, we can also see some striking commonality. Goddesses who rule over Faery are usually associated with war and battle, and quite often take a psychopomp role in that they can travel between worlds and guide the souls of the slain on their journey to the underworld. They invariably are considered sorceresses and shapeshifters, with powerful skills in the magickal arts, and usually with similar animal associations, such as ravens, horses, serpents, wolves, or dogs. A gift that these goddesses also seem to have in common is the gift of prophecy, often playing a hand in the fates they predict for mortals. This is particularly interesting when we consider that the name *faery* comes from the Latin *fata*, meaning "fate."

The Ancestors and Spirits of the Dead

> *"In the Western Isles of Scotland the Sluagh, or fairy*
> *host, was regarded as composed of the souls of the dead*
> *flying through the air, and the feast of the dead at*
> *Hallowe'en was likewise the festival of the fairies."*
>
> Lewis Spence, *The Magic Arts in Celtic Britain*

· · · · · · ·

Faeries and the spirits of the dead have long been associated in Celtic folklore and mystical belief. Whereas most see the faeries as a race of beings in their own right, they are undeniably connected to the realm of the dead, and there are some who believe them to be one and the same. The sidhe of Ireland are named for the same burial mounds in which the ancestors rest, and the Banshee, or Bean-Sidhe (Faery Woman), who gives an eerie scream into the night when a member of a particular family is about to die, is often referred to as a ghost or ancestral spirit. Folklore is replete with tales of departed relatives being sighted in the company of faeries, and there are numerous mentions of precognitive visions of this nature, with the person spotted in the company of the faeries dying a short time afterwards.

Akin to the belief that Faery beings may, in fact, be the spirits of the restless dead is the theory that they are a memory of our ancient ancestors, who lived in turf-covered homes and were short and dark. Perhaps in some cases this may be true, and this memory has been passed down through folklore. Indeed, some places may hold strong memories of earlier times and people that we may witness as echoes in the energy of the land, but this theory comes nowhere near to explaining the wide variety of beings that may be encountered within Faery, nor the powers that they undoubtedly hold.

As to the association with days such as Samhain, a festival in which the dead may be invited to feast with us and share their tales, this also is no clear evidence for faeries being interchangeable with the ancestors or recently deceased, but, again, it does show a connection. Both faeries and the dead dwell on the other side of the veil, between the worlds, where all is mysterious to us. At times such as Samhain, other cross-quarter days, and the solstices and equinoxes, the veil grows thin, and visions of both Faery and the spirits of the dead are more likely.

If indeed they inhabit the same realm, is it any wonder they are sometimes seen together? It has already been noted that many goddesses who are also Faery queens rule over both Faery and the dead, but it is not implied that they are the same. It makes sense that if a queen is ruling a realm, she will rule all the inhabitants of that realm, even if their natures are different. As R. J. Stewart, the respected teacher of Faery tradition, notes, "There is a crossover between the idea of the dead and the faery beings, but they really are quite distinct—the key thing being that the faery beings have never been human…"

Another notable difference is that generally once a spirit has passed over, they will not return to the land of the living, whereas Faery beings have the ability to pass between worlds as they wish. Most instances of "ghosts" are either energetic recordings imprinted on the atmosphere or restless dead who have not passed over for some reason.

Spiritual contact via mediums with those who have passed over can be compared to shamanic work, with the medium being literally that: a mediator between the worlds. Considering the nature of Faery and how we perceive energetically through a number of filters, including memory, preconceived ideas, and other impressions from around us, it seems very possible that we might, for instance, see trooping faeries appear as soldiers in period uniform if a battle took place where there is also faery activity. This may well add to the confusion between the two!

It is an accepted part of Faery lore that human souls may be taken into Faery after death (or sometimes physically whilst still alive), so we may well encounter human spirits acting as guides or envoys in our dealings with Faery. This is often the case if someone has had a strong interest and connection with Faery in life, as with the Reverend Robert Kirk, who was famously taken into Faery in 1692 and has been seen in vision and meditation by many since as an otherworldly envoy. It is also a considerable possibility, therefore, that Faery beings may take the journey in the other direction and be born into human bodies.

These are all mysteries from which we may receive insights, fleeting visions, and flashes of inspiration, but the ultimate knowledge remains obscured. Our astral selves may pay a fleeting visit to the otherworld in journey, meditation, or dreams, but we will never truly experience it until we ourselves fully pass over, as those who walk between the worlds must always keep one foot on solid ground. However, through the contact that we do have, we can easily ascertain that though there is indeed a strong connection, there is much more to Faery beings than simply the departed souls of humans and our ancestors.

Aliens

A very modern theory about the origin of Faery beings is that they are actually visitors from another world (as opposed to the otherworld). Advocates of this theory propose that before the days of science fiction, moon landings, and television, the only explanation people could think of for strange lights in the sky and strange-looking people with unusual clothing is that they were a race of magickal beings, i.e., faeries.

There are many intriguing parallels. Crop circles are associated with both faeries dancing and with UFOs landing, though whether either of these is actually responsible is difficult to say. Descriptions of alien sightings often fit exactly with certain kinds of Faery beings, from slender, delicate, and almond-eyed to extremely large and hairy! Also, there is the frequently reported "loss of time" phenomenon, a well-known symptom of Faery contact, and, of course, abduction, which is a huge part of both ancient Faery folklore and the modern folklore of alien visitation. Interestingly, many sightings of UFOs report that they originated not in the sky but from under the ground or the sea.

In fact, this theory is of much more interest when looked at the other way around. Although in this vast and unknowable universe it is not impossible that we would be visited by sentient beings from another world, from what we already know of Faery we can easily see that many modern sightings of aliens and UFOs could, in fact, be Faery experiences. Since Faery beings often take their appearance from the human mind, in addition to the filters within the mind that influence how one perceives energy beings, it is highly possible that in these times of technology and popular science fiction, a Faery being could be interpreted as an alien visitation.

Perhaps both explanations have some truth in them. Who is to say we are not perhaps sometimes visited by the astral forms of Faery beings from other worlds? Or, indeed, that the many instances of similar occurrences may all have different origins and explanations? There are many mysteries in this world.

There are a number of respected authors who claim that ancient civilisations were visited by ancient astronauts, who brought with them knowledge of stellar cartography. The Dogon people of Mali, which is in Western Africa, claim to have been visited in ancient times by tribes from among the stars, who taught them much about mathematics and the movements of the stars and planets. Early accounts of the Tuatha de Danann's arrival in Ireland talk of them arriving in flying ships or great clouds, so if you believe in alien visitation, it is not such a wild theory. Certainly the idea that the Faery race that dwells in the earth has cosmic origins is a very ancient one, with its roots in Celtic folklore.

Fallen Angels

*"Not of the seed of Adam are we, nor is Abraham our father;
but of the seed of the Proud Angel, driven forth from Heaven."*

W. Y. Evans-Wentz, *The Fairy-Faith in Celtic Countries*

• • • • • • •

Celtic folklore tells us that faeries are the angels who were pulled down with Lucifer when he left heaven and were unable to return, the doors to heaven being shut after them to prevent any more angels from following. Since they did not wish to live in hell either, they made a home in earth's hollow places. Since this lore is passed down through obviously biased Christian priests, to whom the Faery race were, for the most part, devils and at best to be pitied, it is easy to dismiss this origin theory as being simply anti-Pagan propaganda. It is interesting to note, however, that there is a very similar tale within Muslim culture of the origin of the djinn, a race of fiery, airy beings who are the Arabic equivalent of the faerie race and the origin of the wish-granting genie we are all familiar with. When God orders the angels in heaven to bow down and worship the newly created man, the leader of the angels, Iblis (the Islamic equivalent to Lucifer), refuses and is cast out to become the leader of the Shaytan, the race of fallen djinn from whom the name *Satan* derives.

There are undeniable connections between the angel, demon, and Faery races, and if we can free ourselves from prejudice and preconceptions and approach the subject with a curious and open mind, we can learn much of the deeper mystical nature of our Faery cousins and their function within the world and the cosmos.

On the most obvious level, the parallels are clear. Both Faery beings and angels are powerful, shining beings, possessed of their own inner source of luminescence. Both are credited as being sources of inspiration and are particularly associated with inhumanly beautiful music and dancing, and they are both most popularly portrayed and perceived as winged beings. Angels and Faery beings both have a resonance with the light of the stars, though the angels are seen to dwell there, whereas the Faery race dance beneath the stars and sing to them, and emit something of that stellar power into our green world. This takes us into a deeper level and adds some spiritual credence to the fallen angel theory.

Lisa Hunt, "Djinn"; www.lisahuntart.com
(reproduced with kind permission
of US Games Systems, Inc.)

Looking beyond the Judeo-Christian and Islamic religious framework and see-ing the Faery and angelic races as beings of cosmic energy who are far older than any human theological concept, if angels are the agents of cosmic energies and messengers of a spiritual source from above, then Faery beings can be seen as angels of the inner earth, having brought that energy from the source down into the centre of the earth, breathing spiritual life into its centre and now radiating that energy outwards from within, connecting the earth to the web of the universe and enabling sentient spiritual life to evolve. It must not be overlooked that the core of our planet itself radiates its own cosmic energy—it is the star within our earth that illuminates the otherworld.

The name *Lucifer* means "light bringer," so returning to the folklore with the added dimension gained by looking beyond it, we can see the wisdom hidden behind the dogma. If "God" is, in fact, the source of spiritual light, then Lucifer is, in fact, the agent of this light sent to earth. There are also parallels, therefore, between Jesus (as the son of God sent to earth to redeem humankind) and the fall of Lucifer, which, though seem-ingly straying from the subject of Faery Craft, gives interesting food for thought. (Quite literally food for thought when we consider Lucifer's connection to the apple of the Tree of Knowledge, which first brought wisdom to humanity, and how the primal beauty of Faery can be compared to the Garden of Eden.)

The Reverend Robert Kirk, who was both a man of God and one who truly loved the Faery race, observed in his indispensable *The Secret Commonwealth of Elves, Fauns, and Fairies* that they "are said to be of a middle nature betwixt man and angel." By their very nature as spirits connected to earth, they are indeed closer to us than the cosmic energy of angels. Within the same work he also observed the great sadness that is an undeniable part of the nature of Faery, which is the shadow that lives alongside the light of their abundant joy: "Some say that their continual sadness is because of their pendulous state, as uncertain what at the last revolution will become of them."

By the "last revolution" he means the day of the Last Judgment, when it is said that the sidhe are expecting salvation, at last able to return to their celestial origins at the end of days. Again, in the context of Faery beings as being spiritual forces of inner earth, this makes sense, as if life on earth did, indeed, end, they would return to the source. However, there are other possible interpretations. If we interpret the many omens of Judgment Day as being the herald of a new stage in our spiritual evolution as opposed to an ending, then it may be that these prophecies, in fact, refer to a time when Faery will be seen again on the surface of the world.

Returning to Evans-Wentz's *Fairy-Faith in Celtic Countries*, there are several accounts that hint at this possibility, stating that "before the consummation of the world they will be seen as numerous as ever." Since these predictions are accompanied by similar biblical images such as the dead rising from the grave and angels being seen on earth, it is not a huge stretch of the imagination to suggest that instead of the dead literally crawling out of graves (no doubt to feed on our brains), if humanity's awareness were expanded, we would become more aware of all the invisible spiritual beings around us. This includes not only the ancestors but Faery as well.

On the deepest level this refers to an awakening in humanity as a result of the awakening of the inner light of the planet itself. In John Matthews's fascinating contemporary account of Faery contact, *The Sidhe: Wisdom from the Celtic Otherworld*, he receives an insight from the sidhe that hints at this very possibility: "We believe that a new era may be about to dawn in which the people of the sidhe will come forth again and be seen by all."

Through examining the possible origin of Faery beings as fallen angels, we gain insight into not only Faery but also ourselves as spiritual beings and our relationship and connection to them. They, like us, are both of earth and stars. Like us, their spiritual origins are in the cosmos. As those of us on a spiritual path long for reconnection with the cosmic source of spirit, so do the Faery beings. They are our cousins in spirit.

World Soul

"The nymphs of the fountains and all the water-spirits and the depths of the earth and the air and the gleaming hollows are the lunar riders and the rulers of matter, celestial, starry, and that which is of the abysses."

Chaldean Oracles

• • • • • •

The ideas discussed here of Faery as being originally cosmic energy that now radiates from inner earth have direct and fascinating parallels with the ancient concept of the world soul, which exists in a number of ancient worldviews in slightly varying forms and still resonates today as a cosmic truth. The phrase *world soul* originates with the ancient Greek philosopher Plato, but similar concepts that predate his writings can be found around the world in ancient Egypt, the beliefs of ancient Semitic tribes, Hindu teachings, and the Chaldean Oracles, mysterious fragments of a collection of writings thought to date back to ancient Babylon. These ancient philosophies essentially tell us that all living things are imbued with spirit that radiates from one source at the centre of earth, which in turn was placed there by a creator god at the beginning of time.

This world soul is usually referred to as female and is the common origin of many wisdom goddesses throughout history, including the Judeo-Christian wisdom goddess the Shekinah, whose presence in Christianity is better known as the Holy Spirit. The earliest origins of this wisdom goddess can be traced back to Sumerian myths of the goddess Inanna some four thousand years before the birth of Christianity. In a fascinating parallel to the tale of the fall of Lucifer, Inanna, also known as the Queen of Heaven, flees from her father's heavenly realm to bring wisdom to humanity. It is also extremely interesting to note that both Inanna and her Semitic equivalent Astarte are worshipped as the Morning Star, the title of the planet Venus, which is also associated with Lucifer. It is also interesting to note that Innana and Astarte are both associated with the septagram that has in recent years been closely linked to Faery as the "elven star."

Later manifestations of the wisdom goddess, most notably the Gnostic Sophia, also strongly feature the theme of light that "falls" into the world to bring wisdom to the earthly realm. I will not dwell too long on this area but will draw your attention to more interesting parallels for consideration that may deepen your understanding of the nature of Faery. As David Rankine and Sorita D'Este point out in their excellent study *The Cosmic Shekinah*, "The Shekinah is the primordial light of creation, the heavenly glory of divine wisdom, and the inspiration for prophecy," and this certainly seems relevant to the exploration of Faery. Not only are there the links we have already discussed with Faeries as beings of the light of the inner realm, but there is an interesting connection again with the gift of prophecy, which, as previously discussed, is one of the most constant gifts of Faery, particularly of Faery queens.

Is it coincidental that the goddess Hekate, who in British folklore counts "Faery queen" among her many titles, is also a light bringer and ancient wisdom goddess? Hekate is worshipped as the World Soul as Hekate Soteira (saviour), so this opens up a new area of study and contemplation. Another fascinating aspect of the Shekinah is that she is said to manifest as the Garden of Eden itself. This is another direct connection with Faery, for not only does their ageless realm resemble all descriptions of the perfection inherent in Eden, but a tale from Icelandic folklore tells that the Faery race were, in fact, the children of Eve whom she hid from the eyes of God out of shame, who were then forever cursed by God to remain hidden from sight, gaining the name *Huldufólk*, or "hidden folk." This has obvious similarities with the Celtic tales of faeries as fallen angels and similarly compelling implications when we look at the spiritual truths behind the dogma.

When we work with Faery and visit their realm, we are collaborating with agents of this "primordial light" in order to strengthen the much-needed link between their wisdom and our material world. If we perceive angels as the intermediaries between ourselves and the divine source above, it follows that Faery beings, as "fallen" angels, are the intermediaries between ourselves and the divine source below, or within the world of nature. In a parallel with the loss of the Divine Feminine through mainstream patriarchal religions, our ability to recognise the inherent spirit and wisdom in the world of nature has been weakened. The very light that dwells within the inner world and within the realm of Faery as intermediaries is the source of the same divine spark that dwells within each of us and within every living thing. Through this light, we are all connected.

Faery Hierarchy

When studying the Faery realm in any depth, it becomes apparent that beneath the seeming chaos, just as in nature, there is order. The hierarchy of Faery has not been as well documented as that of their upperworld angelic counterparts, but fragments may be found throughout folklore, and through experience and interaction with a variety of Faery beings, a certain clear hierarchy emerges.

There are, of course, the kings and queens of Faery, who are often associated with dominant features in the landscape such as mountains or great hills. Below that, we have the lords and ladies, the gentry, or the trooping faeries, who, as their names suggest, could be considered the Faery nobility, though it is worth considering whether any of this is simply their way of trying to make themselves understood to humanity by mimicking our own social structures of the past. However, if we look at great shining beings such as the sidhe, they are so different in power and ability from, for example, a dryad (tree spirit), that there is a definite hierarchical quality. This is not to say that even the most seemingly limited Faery being, elemental, or nature spirit should ever be underestimated. Within these "lordly" classes of Faery beings there are many tribes and roles, and these vary from area to area, as may be seen in tales and experiences around the world, yet there are always parallels to be found. For want of a better word, the "lower" classes of Faery beings are more accurately referred to as nature spirits, and below that, the elementals of earth, air, fire, and water (i.e., gnomes, sylphs, salamanders, and undines).

The grimoire magicians of the Renaissance were well aware of the existence of a hierarchy within the Faery realm and made good use of it within their work:

> I exorcise, adjure, call upon and Earnestly Require you terrestrial spirits, that are the supreme head of the hierarchy, of those that are called Fairies, and who are called by the names of Mycob and Oberyon…to command the seven sisters Lilia, Rostilia, Foca, Folia, Africa, Julia, Venulla, or some one of them to appear visibly to us…(the seventeenth-century Sloane MS 3824, as quoted in David Rankine's *Book of Treasure Spirits*, 2009)

They used very similar techniques to conjure Faery beings as they did to conjure demons and angels, primarily in order to locate buried treasure troves! Interestingly, though, instead of the usual threatening behaviour, Faery beings would be bribed with a good meal of "a chicken or any kind of small joint, or piece of meat handsomely roasted" (Ibid.), so it is clear that the magicians were aware that Faery beings could not be controlled in the usual methods and must be appealed to instead.

The author and teacher R. J. Stewart has been studying Faery tradition for over thirty years, and I asked him in a recent interview about his experiences of Faery hierarchy:

> I have described it in several of my books, especially *Earth Light*, *Power Within the Land*, and *The Well of Light*. It's very easy to understand, because it starts with huge beings who are of, say, the Atlantic or the Pacific, or of the European landmass, so it's a total consciousness like that, which is what the Greeks would have called Titans. Inside them, you have lesser (but still very large) beings that are of the mountains or forests—they're like a massive consciousness of the forest or the river. Then, inside that, you have somewhat smaller ones like a mountain, a region. Then, eventually, just as in the human world, you get the smaller inhab-

itants who live in that region, the difference being that these are all consciousness. They're not just geography, they're consciousness. Places, People, and Powers are the three Ps to remember.

This is a fascinating way of looking at hierarchy within Faery, more like a Russian doll than a pyramid, with the smaller beings contained within the energies of the larger landscape spirits. Of course, this also works with the idea of the world soul, as all beings would then be contained within the greater planetary spirit.

Unseelie, or the Darker Side of Faery

"We remember the elves for their beauty and the way they move and forget what they were. We're like mice saying 'Say what you like, cats have got real style'…"

Terry Pratchett, Lords and Ladies

• • • • • • •

It is extremely important to understand when working towards connection with Faery and cooperation with their realm that not all Faery beings want to work with us. Most of us are lucky enough not to encounter directly negative attention from Faery, as most who do not wish to work with us simply wish to be left alone, and this wish should certainly be respected. Others amongst them may be termed unseelie—a term from Scottish Faery lore that translates as "unholy," as opposed to their polarity, the seelie, or "blessed," court. Religious connotations aside, these are the beings whose solution to the problems of the world would be to simply get rid of humans if given the chance. An excellent portrayal of this in recent popular culture can be seen in the hit movie *Hellboy* II, which also succeeds in making their viewpoint quite understandable.

Scotland is not the only place to draw a clear distinction between the dark and the light courts of Faery. In the Nordic myths there were light and dark elves, or alfar and svartalfar, who lived in Alfheim and Svartalfheim, respectively. In South Africa, where there is a strong belief in Faery beings, they raise the beds of children from the floor to protect from the dangerous tokoloshe. Almost all the Slavic faeries are considered extremely malevolent, and Native American culture has its harmful spirits also, who cause disease and famine.

Emily Carding, "Svartalfheim"

Indeed, most countries have their Faery races, and within them may always be found purely malicious beings. You will most likely not encounter these beings, but if you do, treat them with courtesy and respect and do all you can to keep them at a distance. It is important to understand that they cannot be reasoned with. If necessary, iron may be used, but only as a last resort—and it will also drive away most other Faery beings. Bear in mind this may offend them, and they have long memories.

Truthfully, any Faery being is dangerous when crossed, to different extents, according to their natures. Who is to say that those we call unseelie do not have good reason to be, from some past betrayal? That is why it is so important to always be honourable in our dealings with all otherworldly (and, indeed, this-worldly) beings, for applying certain rules in some cases and not in others, or neglecting to live by our spiritual principles in daily life, does not a true and clear path make.

Faery Etiquette

Unfortunately, amidst the modern prevalence for quick fixes and doing "whatever feels right" in the modern magickal community, the ancient rules of Faery etiquette, which are woven throughout our myths and folklore, have been much neglected. However, they are highly relevant and ignored at our peril!

Iron

The prohibition against iron is well known, and there are a number of differing theories as to its origins and reasoning. It has been suggested that it is man's use of iron in weapons, bringing an end to the Bronze Age, which originally drove the Faery race beneath the hollow hills and beyond the veil. This may have some truth in it, but the simple fact is that iron has the power to hurt all spiritual creatures, not only Faery beings. This is why magicians use a sword containing iron to control summoned entities.

It is considered extremely rude to carry iron tools or use them in Faery Craft, and for this reason steel is to be avoided also. When cutting any plants or trees for Faery work, a sharp knife of bronze, stone, or bone is preferable, and this must also be with agreement from the spirit of the plant. There are several exercises within this book designed to strengthen connection to the point where communication of this sort should be possible with practice. There is, however, no need to be paranoid about iron content in metal to the extent that you worry about belt buckles and underwired bras!

Taking from Sacred Sites and Trees

One of the chief causes of anger amongst the Faery realm against humanity is our propensity for taking without the thought of asking or giving fair exchange in return. This is another reason for working on connection and intuition before all else, so that we develop a strong sense of when a site or tree is sacred. Not all places that are sacred are marked in obvious ways, and certainly not those places that are sacred to Faery and beyond the ken of humanity. Permission must always be asked from the spirits of place before working on their land, and nothing must be taken from the area without explicit permission. There are well-documented accounts in folklore of ill-fated men cutting down Faery trees (usually thorns) or even taking branches from them, and then being stricken with serious illness and even death. Moving sacred stones also elicits similar punishment:

There was a man on the road between Chevy and Marble Hill, where there is a faery plumb-stone that stands straight up and it about five feet in height, and the man was building a house and carried it away to put above his door. And from the time he brought it away, all his stock began to die, and whenever he went in or out, night or day, he was severely beaten. So at last he took the stone down and put it back where it was before, and from that time nothing has troubled him. (Lady Gregory, *Visions and Beliefs in the West of Ireland*)

In fact, in November 2011, there was a report in an Irish newspaper of a wealthy man who lost all his fortune reputedly because he had removed an ancient burial mound from his land. The headline read SEAN QUINN'S DOWNFALL IS FAIRIES' REVENGE, a clear sign that belief in the ancient Faery lore is alive and well!

Thanking

There is a curious piece of Faery lore that says we should never thank them for things they do for us. This is seen in a number of tales, where being thanked or given payment of any kind results in the faerie leaving and never being seen again. It is my personal opinion that this is down to misunderstanding on both sides, and that simply giving thanks without following reciprocal action can be seen as being dismissive. We should indeed be grateful but show our gratitude through continued cooperation and team-work rather than thanking and drawing the alliance to a close.

Lying

Lying is very simply unacceptable—to them, to ourselves, and to others. Equally important is the keeping of promises, as failure to keep a promise is a form of lying. Faery beings will always know, and they will have no dealings with those who have the shadow of deception upon their heart.

Offerings

There are a number of important considerations to bear in mind concerning the very important area of offerings, and these are covered in great detail in chapter 4: Honour.

Eating Faery Food

Most people have heard the prohibition against consuming food or drink from the land of Faery, and it is right to be wary. It is important to spend many years working on connection and building up experience to be able to judge when this particular rule may be broken.

Faery Beasts

"She turned about her milk-white steed,
And took True Thomas up behind,
And aye whene'er her bridle rang,
The steed flew swifter than the wind…"

Thomas Rhymer, traditional Scottish ballad

· · · · · · ·

There are a number of animals that seem to have special significance or connection to the Faery realm and its inhabitants. Often their appearance in our world heralds the presence of other Faery beings, sometimes the beginning of an adventure into the Faery realm, or in some cases they may be Faery beings themselves in borrowed or shifted form. Often there is some distinctive physical characteristic that betrays their other-worldly natures. Often Faery beasts are either completely white, completely black, or white with a striking touch of red, such as the hounds of Annwn, who are bright white with blood-red ears. The colours black, white, and red are sacred to Faery. They are alchemical colours that, amongst other things, represent the cycle of life, death, and rebirth; the rivers of blood and tears that flow through the Celtic underworld; and the triple realms of upperworld, underworld, and middleworld.

Horse

A majestic white horse, often bedecked with many bells, is the traditional steed of Faery queens. Horses are particularly associated with the Celtic goddesses Rhiannon, Epona, the Morrigan, and the Greek Hekate, who is sometimes depicted as having three animal heads upon one body, one of which is a horse. All of these goddesses may be considered to be queens of Faery, alongside many other titles in some cases. Horses are also the companions of Faery kings, of course. Manannan Mac Lir had a magickal horse

Marc Potts, "Pixy and Skylark"
(www.marcpotts.co.uk)

that could carry people over the waves and deep into his otherworldly kingdom beneath the sea.

Horses often appear as Faery beings in their own right, such as the kelpie, a lethally dangerous and malicious spirit of water who drowns any who climb on its back, and of course the beautiful symbol of spiritual perfection and purity, the unicorn.

Folklore aside, horses are extremely intelligent and magickally sensitive creatures and will often act as guardians. The landscape of the British Isles is blessed by many chalk figures of horses carved into the landscape. They are of varying age, but some, such as the famous white horse at Uffington, have been shown to date back to the Bronze Age and possibly even further. These are truly sacred sites, where the veil between worlds is thin and may offer you a glimpse of a gleaming white mare dancing elusively in the dusk…

Birds

Birds have long been associated with the Faery realm, most particularly black birds, such as ravens, crows, and, of course, blackbirds. In The Book of Invasions, Eochaid, the son of the high king, receives a prophetic dream that predicts the arrival into Ireland of the Tuatha de Danann, in which he sees them as a flock of blackbirds. The shapeshifting goddess Morrigan, who as we have already noted is a Faery queen, is strongly associated with ravens and crows, often taking their form. The goddess Rhiannon, another Faery queen, was accompanied by blackbirds who had the power of enchanted song. As blackbirds can be heard singing at the liminal times of dawn and dusk, when faerie activity is most apparent, they are considered to be gatekeepers of the otherworld.

Cows

Within Faery lore there are both cows that are very much independent Faery beings in themselves and those that are simply property. In the ancient tales of the Tuatha de Danann, the Cattle Raid of Cooley was a major campaign, caused by the trickery of the goddess Morrigan. This extremely cow-oriented adventure also features the Morrigan taking the form of a white heifer with red ears and, later on, as an old woman milking a three-teated Faery cow.

There are also many tales within more recent folklore of faeries taking the milk of cows, causing milk to sour, or making cows' udders dry up when they are wronged or denied in some way.

Pigs

Pigs may seem an unlikely contender for the Faery kingdom, but herds of pigs are a regular feature of the old Celtic tales. Manannan of the Tuatha de Danann owned a herd of pigs that could be slaughtered and eaten one night and be returned to full health the next day. The Norse god Freyr, who was the king of Alfheim (Elf-Home), rode a wild boar named Gullinbursti, who had the power to travel over earth, air, and sea. Myrddin Wylt, the mythical or possibly historical wild man of the woods, from whom the more well-known mythical figure of Merlin arose, counted a pig as one of his close friends of the forest and famously addressed poetry to him.

Insects

It seems obvious to point out that there is a close connection between certain insects and the Faery realm, though there is not a great deal of lore to support this. Faeries are often depicted as riding on the backs of certain insects, particularly dragonflies, ladybirds, and butterflies. Though it would be easy to dismiss this as mere fancy and aesthetic license, and mostly a result of the "flower fairy" mentality, there is some truth to be found in this. To "ride" an animal of any kind is a term that can be used in a Witchcraft context to mean not literally physically riding but to astrally ride alongside the spirit of that animal within its body. In my experience, Faery beings have an intimate relationship with all creatures of this land, which enables them to do this easily, and I believe this explains many instances of unusual behaviour in animals and insects, particularly when guarding or protecting places of power and sacred sites.

I have experienced this phenomenon a number of times with insects, particularly bees, wasps, butterflies, dragonflies, and damselflies. A lovely example occurred whilst in the final stages of working on this book. I had printed out the document and my husband was reading it in the garden when a butterfly landed on the page and stayed there for some time. It landed precisely on a line of the interview with R. J. Stewart that appears later in the book, which states that faeries never appear with "little butterfly wings"! A sense of humour is so important when dealing with Faery.

Dogs

Dogs feature heavily in Faery lore, predominantly as the red-eared white hounds of the otherworld. Known as the Cwn Annwn in Welsh tradition, they would accompany Arawn or Gwyn ap Nudd on their hunts or on Samhain night when the host would ride out, bringing fear to the land. The Tuatha de Danann and the Fomorians also had hounds; in fact, the name of the great hero of the Tuatha, Cu Chulainn, means "hound of Chulainn."

There is a strong tradition of strange black dogs associated with Faery in England that is almost interchangeable with stories of ghosts and ill omens. The goddess Hekate is also associated with black dogs. They were sacrificed to her in ancient Greece at the crossroads, and in her triple-animal-headed form she would often have the head of a dog. This may be seen to relate to her underworld aspect as Hekate Chthonia, which logically would be the aspect most connected to the Faery realm. Much of the folklore connected to black dogs in England also connects them to the crossroads, generally as the lost souls of hanged criminals.

The wild relatives of dogs, wolves and foxes, also have strong connections with Faery lore worldwide. Foxes are particularly apparent in Chinese folklore in the form of shape-shifting femme fatales known as huli jing, and also in Japan, where they are known as kitsune.

Deer

Deer, both hinds and stags, are an important part of Faery lore. In Celtic myth, it is often a white stag or hind that leads the way to the otherworld or lures unsuspecting huntsmen. Faery beings sometimes take the guise of deer, and Faery kings are often depicted as having the antlers of a stag. To be transformed into a deer for a span of time is also a punishment inflicted on mortals in a number of tales.

Cats

Katharine Briggs states that "cats were almost fairies in themselves" (A *Dictionary of Fairies*), and I'm sure that most cat lovers would agree! They certainly have otherworldly qualities. There is also a tradition of Faery cats in Scotland known as cait sith, and a number of people have suggested that the phantom big cats sometimes sighted on British moorland, such as the Beast of Bodmin, may, in fact, be Faery cats.

There is also an increased reporting in recent years of "shadow cats," which are cat-size shadowy creatures that have been seen to pass through walls and into impossible spaces. These may well be a form of Faery being.

Serpents

As ancient chthonic symbols, serpents often arise in Faery lore. There are a number of beings who are described as being part serpent, such as the Faery bride Melusine. You may not realise it, but you see an image of Melusine every time you pass a Starbucks.

Mythical Beasts

There are a large number of mythical beasts associated with Faery, and we do not have room for an entire bestiary within this volume! Many of these may be encountered when working in the Faery realm either in journey, meditation, or other work in an altered state. Dragons, like Faery beings, are agents of the deepest powers of inner earth and the elements, and they may be encountered in wild landscapes and high, rugged places where the primal power of the land may be felt. Unicorns, beautiful symbols of purity and spirit, are also often seen in vision.

Esther Remmington, "Earth Dragon"
(www.estherremmington.com)

TOP: **septagram** BOTTOM, FROM LEFT: four-leaved
clover, pentagram, triskele, equal-armed cross
RIGHT: the great glyph of the sidhe

Symbols

Symbols are not an obvious or traditional part of Faery Craft, which is mostly concerned with the world of nature and the otherworld; however, there are a number of symbols that have particular associations relevant to Faery. Symbols change and evolve in their meaning over time, and if you wish to add your own personal significance and insights to those mentioned here, that is completely acceptable as long as they resonate with the symbol's innate energy. As you will see below, many of the associations connected with these symbols are surprisingly recent, and they all hold a number of equally relevant meanings.

Septagram

The seven-pointed star known as a septagram or heptagram is used by many people who walk a Faery path to represent their beliefs, where it is known as the Faery Star or Elven Star. However, this is a very recent usage of this ancient symbol, originating in the 1980s with the Elf Queen's Daughters, a group originating in the hippie movement of 1970s California who believed themselves to be elves incarnated into human form to help guide the planet towards peaceful ways. This inspired many to "awaken" to their own natures as incarnated magickal beings, such as the Silver Elves (who are interviewed later in this book) and the Otherkin movement that emerged in the 1990s and use the septagram as their identifying symbol.

One of the oldest uses of this star is to represent the sphere of Venus and the power of love within the Qabalah. It can also be found within Christian tradition as a symbol of protection, representing the perfection of God, hence its appearance (inverted) on some sheriff's badges in the States.

The recent nature of its association with Faery does not, however, detract from its significance in this role. The number seven and things of a sevenfold nature are deeply significant in understanding the patterns of the world and the otherworld. It is fascinating to note that in most accounts from folklore of people being taken away to Faery, it is for a period of seven months or seven years, and through ancient myths the number seven constantly occurs in matters relating to Faery.

Not only can the septagram represent the seven planets, the seven days of the week, and the seven colours of the rainbow, but it can also stand for the seven directions that we use in our work with Faery and other paths that acknowledge the importance of above, below, and within. It has been used as such in the structure of this book, taking as the chapter headings seven qualities needed in Faery Craft, which correspond to the seven points of the star, the directions, and the elements. For this purpose, the points have been labeled sun, moon, stars, earth, air, fire, and water. The sun in this case represents the inner light of self, the within, and the quality of honour. The moon represents the below and magick, the stars represent the above and connection, earth is trust, air is knowledge, fire is inspiration, and water is joy. As the book progresses you will grow to understand not only why these qualities are so important but how they relate to the directions, as well as how they relate to the contents of the book.

The sacred number three can also be found within the mathematical pattern of this star, as when it is drawn point to point, every third point connects. This shows that though its use as a sacred symbol within Faery traditions is extremely recent, the relevance is inherent within its very structure.

Pentagram

The five-pointed star, or pentagram, has become very recognisable as a symbol of Pagan beliefs, most particularly Wicca-based paths. Within this context it represents the balance and power of the five elements of earth, air, fire, water, and spirit, and it is used for both invoking and banishing the powers of these elements, as well as for protection. However this symbol has been in use for many thousands of years and by many different cultures.

The Pythagoreans, to whom it symbolised mathematical perfection, used the pentagram as a secret symbol by which to identify each other. They identified the five points of the star with the five elements, which continues to this day. Though many Christians may look down upon this symbol due to its overuse in kitschy horror flicks as well as its association with Pagan and magickal paths, early Christians actually saw the pentagram as symbolic of the five wounds of Christ and a sacred symbol of universal truth.

Though the earliest evidence of this symbol can be found in ancient Babylonian pottery fragments from 3500 BCE, in truth this symbol has been with us since the evolution of life. The mathematical pattern it encapsulates is seen throughout the natural world—in flowers, in the core of an apple, even in our own bodies. Of course the innate relationship with the elements and perfection in nature gives this symbol great relevance in Faery Craft, as does its effectiveness as a symbol of protection.

One more fascinating detail is its use in the Grimoire tradition for summoning Faery beings. The grimoire magicians would use very similar methods to summon Faery beings (normally to help in the hunt for hidden treasure) as they would for angels and demons, only instead of a constraining triangle outside the circle, they would use a pentagram. As grimoire expert David Rankine notes in *Grimoires, Fairies and Treasure*:

> Even then the magicians were sensible enough not to try and apply the same rules to fairies as to demons, recognizing that fairies were already far closer to the physical realm and able to manifest at will rather than needing to be summoned, as was the case for many other spiritual creatures.

Triskele

The triskele or triskelion is an ancient Celtic symbol that can be seen to have many meanings within its obvious triple nature. The name of the symbol translates as "three legged," and indeed, in its form as the Manx flag, the spirals do take on the appearance of legs in motion. We may think of it, then, as a symbol of cycles that never end—the journey of life, death, and rebirth that is constantly in motion. The three spiral arms of the triskele may also be seen to represent the past, present, and future, with the centre showing where we stand in connected awareness of all that is, has been, and will be.

The number three is of great magickal significance and can be seen repeatedly and in many forms in Faery lore. We see it in triple-formed goddesses such as the Morrigan, Hekate, and the Fates themselves; in the triple crossroads, the paths leading to hell, heaven, and elfland; in the traditional three wishes of fairy tales; in the three guesses to the riddle; in the three colours of red, black, and white; in the three realms of land, sea, and sky; and even in the elements of earth, air, and water, with fire being the divine spark that dwells within.

This ancient symbol resembles the patterns of water as they flow around obstacles in a river or the ripples that are sent out when a stone is thrown into a pond. Indeed, spirals can be found throughout nature—from the DNA that carries seemingly impossible amounts of coded information, to the largest galaxy. As above, so below. The world of nature holds much wisdom, and that is reflected in this symbol. We should always remember that we stand in the centre of our own world, sending out ripples of consequence with every action.

Equal-Armed Cross

The equal-armed cross within a circle is the alchemical symbol for earth and is used within Qabalah to represent the material realm of Malkuth. As a symbol for earth, its significance to Faery Craft is obvious, not the least because this symbol actually appears naturally on the Faery stone known as staurolite.

We can also see this symbol as representing the sacred crossroads between the worlds. In Celtic myth and folklore there are many tales of humans and Faery beings meeting at crossroads, such as the Cornish tale about Cherry of Zennor and the famous Scottish ballad about Thomas the Rhymer. It can also be seen as the meeting place of the paths leading to the four cities of Falias, Gorias, Murias, and Finias, which, according to the eleventh-century collection of ancient Irish folklore called The Book of Invasions, are the cities from which the godlike Tuatha de Danann originated. These four cities are connected to the four elements of earth, air, fire, and water and the sacred hallows of the Tuatha de Danann.

This symbol can also be seen to represent balance between the elements and the position of the self as being always in the centre of the directions, protected by the circle. If you think of the symbol as being two lines crossing rather than four lines meeting, then it can be seen as the meeting of two worlds or two polarities (in this case, our world and the otherworld). The worlds are brought together to meet in the cross and brought together in harmony by the circle, an ancient symbol of perfection.

Four-Leaved Clover

The four-leaved clover is nature's own symbol for (or perhaps from) the Faery realm. Though most people know that to find one of these rare mutations is considered to bring good luck, many have forgotten that they are also said to bring the ability to see Faery and herald the presence of nearby Faery beings. In many old tales there is mention of an ointment that enables true sight of the otherworld, including the ability to see through glamour, of which it is said that four-leaved clover is a chief ingredient. In the old tale The Four-Leaved Clover, a milkmaid is given extraordinary vision of mischievous piskies through accidentally placing some in her hat:

> In looking it over by the candlelight she found a bunch of three-leaved grass and one stem with four leaves. She knew it was no strange thing that she should see the Small People… (Hunt, Popular Romances of the West of England).

Conversely, this rare gem of the natural world is also said to bring protection from the faeries. We can interpret from both these meanings that the four-leaved clover gives one a certain amount of power within and over Faery. It is also interesting to note that from above, the four-leaved clover resembles the equal-armed cross surrounded by a circle.

The Great Glyph of the Sidhe

> *"I dreamed I was back under the mound of Gortnasheen,*
> *which seemed as if lit by flickering candlelight. I stood before*
> *the glyph, which glowed as if lit from within, unable to tear my*
> *eyes from its shape. Then slowly I became aware of a figure…"*

John Matthews, *The Sidhe*

· · · · · · ·

Symbols can be extremely effective gateways, and one especially suited for connection to the land and beings of Faery is the great glyph of the sidhe. This symbol was first brought to public attention by the author John Matthews in his channeled work *The Sidhe: Wisdom from the Celtic Otherworld*, but it has been in use by certain practitioners for some time. This labyrinthian spiral provides a simple yet extremely potent method for communicating with Faery beings and for visiting their land. There is no prescribed method of use, nor is there any guided element to the result. By providing this symbol, I am merely presenting a door through which you may choose to pass, and all visions and insights will be your own, authentic and unique to you.

EXERCISE: *The Great Glyph of Sidhe Meditation*

If this is a method you wish to try, I recommend painting the image yourself onto a canvas of reasonable size, thus imbuing it with your own energy as well as giving you a clear image large enough to use for meditation. You may wish to light a candle on either side of the image, as John Matthews suggests in his work.

Simply sit comfortably in calm surroundings and allow the symbol to become ingrained in your vision. When you can confidently see the symbol in your mind's eye, close your eyes and see the spiral becoming a tunnel stretching out before you, through which you can pass. Remember to act with courtesy to all beings you might meet and to act only with truth and honour and be grateful for any gifts or wisdom received. Afterwards you may wish to make notes or drawings of any further gateway symbols received. The glyph can work both ways, so you may find beings coming through it to greet you.

I have a piece of slate upon which I have painted the glyph in gold acrylic that forms part of my outdoor Faery shrine. It can also be incorporated into artwork to bring it into greater circulation and strengthen the bridge between worlds, as I did in my own *Tarot of the Sidhe*.

Suggested Activities

Research

Spend some time researching the area where you live. If you have moved areas or even countries during your life, as so many of us in the modern world have, also learn about where you were born. If you're not sure where to start, try your local library and the Internet. Are there any traditional sacred sites? Any wells or springs? Any trees or areas of woodland with significance or lore attached to them? What are the stories of these places? Also look into your own ancestry if possible. What are the traditions of your ancestors? Do any of your relatives have any tales of Faery contact or strange happenings?

Create

Which of the symbols do you feel most drawn to? Practice drawing all the different symbols and see which seems to resonate most with you. You don't need to be a great artist! When you have one or more symbols that you feel a connection with, you can paint or embroider it in the colours of you choice, as simply or as elaborately as you like, on a piece of natural material—for example, cloth, wood, clay, glass, or stone. You could, of course, use copper, silver, or gold if you're feeling flash, but other metals may be inappropriate, especially if they contain any amount of iron. You could also use leather, but if using any kind of animal skin, give due thought to the source. The energy of the kind of animal, the life it led, and how it died will all be contained within its skin.

When you have your completed item, take good care of it. You may choose to use it as a focus for meditations or simply keep it in view in a special place, maybe lighting a candle or burning incense near it. This item will become important later on as the centrepiece of your Faery shrine.

Practice

Perform the meditative exercise as suggested on page 43 at least once during this first month, preferably more. This will help to prepare you for later work, building both your connection with the otherworld and your visualising skills.

CHAPTER TWO
Connection

Now that we have started to assimilate some background knowledge and experience, it is time to start building connection. This crucial quality is linked to the direction of above and the stars. The stars represent the wisdom of the Divine, the power of destiny, and our own cosmic origins. We all gaze at the same sky in wonder, and hence the stars connect us all.

In this chapter we will learn about why connection is so important and how to involve all our senses in our Faery work. We will spend time on strengthening and balancing our energy in the Becoming the Faery Tree exercise, as well as learning the importance of the voice as a tool and how to use it. We will spend some time learning about the elements and elemental beings, including contemplations performed out in nature in order to increase our awareness and connection. Then, through exploration of the completely original Faery zodiac, we will apply this understanding of the elements and elemental beings to our own personalities, giving us a stronger idea of where our elemental strengths and weaknesses lie, and what manner of beings we might best collaborate with in our Faery Craft.

Brian Froud, "Connection"
(www.worldoffroud.com)

The Importance of Connection

*"If ordinary people really knew that consciousness and
not matter is the link that connects us with each other
and the world, then their views about war and peace,
environmental pollution, social justice, religious values, and
all other human endeavors would change radically."*

Amit Goswami, *The Self-Aware Universe*

· · · · · · ·

One of the most common questions asked about Faery is how to see them. We live in a very visually oriented culture, so it is only natural that we wish to see with our eyes in order to truly believe. Many understand the elusiveness of Faery beings and believe in them regardless, but even so the emphasis on needing to see and the implication that only a chosen few are allowed to can lead to disappointment or, worse, the desperate creation of illusory experience.

Illusion is a glamorous and tempting slippery slope, and since it creates experiences from the mind that are designed to make us feel better about ourselves, it is a difficult trap to escape. This is why our approach should be to seek to strengthen our connection with the invisible without placing undue emphasis on making it visible. If you were to go out into the woods and desperately try to *see* a faerie, you would be unconsciously closing off the perceptive possibilities of the other senses and their mystical extensions, making it less likely that you would directly experience their energies. On the other hand, if you were to work on all of the senses in heightened awareness and use your energy to reach out and perceive the subtle energies around you, you are, in fact, much more likely to experience those energies, and the experience in time may lead to visual as well as auditory and empathic sensations.

In my experience, the true path to Faery is through the heart, not the eyes or head. If we approach with an open heart, free from distrust and the ravages of scientific cynicism, then we will soon feel the presence of the spirit within the land. When we do see Faery, we see it not simply through our eyes but through our whole selves. We see through our hearts, through all our senses, and through all our experiences in life. Thus Faery beings, being of fluid energy and not tied to linear time and physicality as we are, may take on wildly differing appearances from individual to individual, according not only to their nature and what they wish to communicate but also to our perceptive ability, which can be influenced by preconceived ideas.

To hone this ability, learn to connect and perceive through the heart. When we can allow our hearts to become a clear channel of perception—in other words, get ourselves out of the way—those initial emotive and energetic sensations can be translated into communication and images through our trained visual imaginations and mystical senses. Like any explorative rather than dictated spiritual path, it is a thin line to walk, and we must always keep a check on ourselves so that we do not descend into delusion. However, if we form a strong connection with the land, learn to trust and root our experience in practical results and pure intentions, the path before us will remain clear of illusory weeds.

EXERCISE: *Becoming the Faery Tree*

The following exercise, which can be performed anywhere, is designed to open up your awareness to the flow of energy within your body and your connection to your surroundings. It will enhance not only your sensitivity to the otherworld, as well as the beings that inhabit it, but with repeated practice will also help you to feel rooted as a part of the landscape, bringing balance and control. It can help connect you to any specific sites in which you perform it, creating sacred space around you.

This is a useful exercise to help ground and focus before any magickal work, especially outdoors, and you can incorporate more elements as you become fluent with the procedure. For example, if you are undertaking magickal work within the landscape or at a sacred site, you may wish to incorporate a call to the spirits of the land at the peak of the exercise as your energies open (suggestions for how to go about this may be found elsewhere in the book). You will find a more advanced version of this exercise later in the book, called Walking in Awareness, but it is wise to become familiar with this simple yet effective version first.

While this may also be performed sitting, standing is preferable. Find a flat and even space to stand, with your feet slightly apart so that you feel strong and stable. If possible, barefoot is best. With your hands by your sides and palms facing down to the ground, focus on your breathing, and use it to calm your mind. As you breathe out, release any worries or tensions of the day. As you breathe in, remember your focus and intent of connection.

If you can, breathe in steadily and deeply for the count of seven, hold for three, and then out again over seven, wait for three, then breathe in again for seven and continue. Three and seven are sacred numbers in Faery Craft. Don't worry if you find this difficult; simply breathe steadily. It will become easier with practice.

Maintaining steady breathing, visualize your feet sinking into the ground. You are as solid and immovable as a tree. From your feet imagine strong roots growing, sinking deep into the ground. Take your time to feel the roots growing and drawing the energy from the ground. You are strong, vital, and stable.

Once you can feel your roots in the earth beneath your feet, keeping your arms straight, slowly raise your hands until they form a V shape above your head.

Remember your breathing—slowly and deeply, in and out.

Keeping your hands raised, imagine your arms as your branches, reaching high into the sky, just as your roots reach deep into the ground. Leafy shoots grow from your fingers and stretch into great tree limbs, strong and graceful.

Hold this image in your mind as you keep your breathing slow, deep, and steady.

When you are ready, with your next breath in, imagine you are drawing light from the inner earth up through your roots. The light and energy moves up your body slowly and surely with each inward breath, through your roots, into your legs, and finally into your torso. Draw the energy up into your heart and feel it opening your energy centre.

Now, holding that energy in your centre, focus on your branches. Feel the light coming from the sky above—the power of the sun and stars—as it flows into you. With every breath, feel the cosmic energy move down through your branches and into your body. Allow the energy from above to meet with the energy of below in your heart. Feel the power of the two forces meeting in your centre, how you are connected to all worlds, bridging the gap between.

Maintain this connection for seven breaths, breathing in for seven, holding for three, and releasing over a count of seven. (With practice, you may hold this longer and use this state for further work.)

When you are ready, release the energy back to the source with every outward breath, first back up through the branches. Once the cosmic energy is released, on your next breath out, slowly lower your arms so that the palms of your hands once more face the floor. As you do so, release the energy back into the ground.

Your energies have now been mixed with both the underworld and upperworld. Give thanks to the powers of place and sit or stand in silence for a while to process your experience. Make any notes you wish when convenient.

The Voice

"Deep as the sea we sing, as high as the moon we sing…"
Emily Carding, *The Song of the Sidhe*

· · · · · · ·

A valuable tool that the vast majority of us have at our disposal is the voice. Voice has the power to carry the energy of emotion or intent into the surroundings, mixing with other sounds and vibrations, echoing off surfaces, instantly connecting our energy with the world around us. Voice can carry the power of words, bringing the internal into outward expression. Be careful that such words are always carefully chosen, for there are always beings who may take meanings literally or intentionally trip you up to teach a lesson! However, allowing wordless song to emerge from our spiritual centre is a powerful way to send out a call to the powers of the inner landscape as well as access our own innate wisdom.

By going out into the wild places and allowing energy to rise out of us as song, we honour the spirits of place as well as announce our intent to commune with them. It's not important to be a strong singer, but it doesn't help to be fearful of being heard. If the note or notes come direct from you and with pure intent, then not only will they will be effective, but in time your voice will become stronger. When we combine this simple technique with journey work and meditation, we can find particular musical phrases and vowel sounds for different tasks. For example, I have a musical phrase that acts as an invocation, calling the sidhe to meet with me. I also have phrases that I use to honour the ancestors, to clear space, or when giving offerings, as well as simply allowing notes to emerge spontaneously as they will. I advise singing to trees, wells, rivers, animals… whenever you feel moved by nature, allow the feeling to emerge through your voice. One day you may hear them singing back to you.

EXERCISE: *Finding Your Voice*

First let the feeling come. You may find it helpful to perform the Faery Tree exercise until the energies are meeting in your centre. Allow your internal focus to settle on the space just below the centre of your rib cage—this is where a sheet of muscle called the diaphragm lies and where your voice needs to be coming from. Try putting your hand over this part of your body and panting lightly to a "ha" sound, and you will feel the muscle working. This muscle is the foundation of your voice. Relax and breathe deeply, breathing right into the full capacity of your lungs and expanding your rib cage. When your rib cage is expanded, your diaphragm has more strength and so is able to lend more support to your voice.

Practice breathing in deeply and releasing your breath slowly with a hissing sound, allowing the breath to exit the bottom of your lungs first, leaving the rib cage expanded until the last of the air is expelled. Now try this again, but with a humming sound. Settle on a note that feels comfortable and resonant within your body. You may feel your back and chest or perhaps even other parts of your body vibrate. When you have found this note, allow your humming to become stronger and increase in volume. This can all happen over as many breaths as you need it to, but remember to take good, deep breaths and keep your rib cage expanded. When you are ready, open your mouth and allow the humming sound to expand into a vowel sound, any vowel sound that comes.

When you are confident in this technique, allow the note and vowel sounds to vary, and you'll soon find yourself bringing through simple and powerful melodies. However, you don't need to use your voice to sing tunes; the act of finding your true resonant note is a powerful exercise in itself. All things in existence vibrate at different frequencies and join together to create the harmony of the song of the universe. By performing this exercise we are consciously joining the song and expressing our true spiritual self.

When you have found your voice, allow it to emerge out in nature, carrying the intent of connection. Picture your voice carrying a golden light from your centre that extends out like a web to touch all the life around you. Know that you are a part of the land and that the land is part of you, and allow your voice to celebrate this knowledge.

The Elements and Elemental Beings

Different cultures around the world have interpreted, categorised, and divided the elements in different ways according to their understanding. The Western Mystery tradition, which is based on the teachings of ancient Greece and Egypt, uses a system of four elements. These elements are air, fire, water, and earth, and they are considered to be the building blocks of physical existence.

Although many Faery beings are often slightly inaccurately referred to in a number of modern works as elementals, like us, they are normally composed of more than one element (although they may show strong inclinations towards one in particular). The true elementals are the spiritual expression of the elements in their purest form. They were first called elementals by the medieval scholar and occultist Paracelsus, but the recognition of spiritual beings of the elements dates back to ancient history. The elementals are not part of the Faery races as such, but connection and awareness of them and the interaction of elements both around and within you are important parts of Faery Craft, as they are an intrinsic part of the natural world. Awareness of the elemental beings, who are immanent and active in our physical realm, can lead to greater awareness of our mutual Faery cousins.

Sylphs

Sylphs are the elementals of air and are often described as taking a beautiful, winged humanoid form. In fact, sylphs are closer in appearance to the popular idea of Faery beings than most faeries themselves! The energy of the sylphs can be most keenly felt in high places, where the earth meets the sky, or in the great winds of a storm. Keeping personal safety in consideration, standing in a storm and allowing the elements to rage around you is a powerful way to feel the presence of these elementals. Sylphs enjoy the sound of woodwind instruments and the human voice, so this is one way you could try to attract their energies. Morning is the most favourable time of day to contact this elemental.

Salamanders

The elementals of fire are known as salamanders, yet they should not be confused with their physical amphibian counterparts. Though they have been known to take reptilian, almost draconic, form, they can appear in various guises. You may experience

Laura Daligan, "The Lady of the Lake"
(www.lauradaligan-art.com)

them as sparks, tongues or balls of fire, or even as I once did: as incredibly ornate wings with beautiful patterns of fiery colours.

Open your awareness whilst standing in the presence of a mighty bonfire to experience the power of these elementals. One way of attracting the attention of salamanders is to sing or play a stringed instrument whilst sitting by the fire or in the midday sun. Something simple, like an Appalachian dulcimer, can make lovely sounds even if you have no musical training. Sometimes simple is best!

Undines

Undines, also known as nymphs, are the elementals of water. Like sylphs, they take the appearance of beautiful humanoids (though wingless) and are generally female and seductive in nature. In folklore there are many tales of their kind interacting with and even marrying humans, this romantic element seeming appropriate for a being that consists entirely of the element associated with our emotions. Since most of the human body is water, perhaps this is why we can relate so intimately with them?

If you can find time to sit by a rushing river or a waterfall, listen and pay close attention to feel the presence of the beautiful undines. If you can sit by water at sunset and play bells or perhaps a singing bowl, this is a good way to attract the attention of undines. Like sylphs, they also love song.

Gnomes

Gnomes are the elementals of earth, and in my experience they are the closest among the elementals to Faery beings, sharing many of the same qualities and in practice being often indistinguishable to the point of wondering why we try to distinguish at all between them. Theirs is the underground realm of soil, stone, and minerals, as well as the roots of growing things. You may experience their presence when spending time in peace and stillness in the roots of a tree surrounded by woodland, or on the side of a mountain where the heartbeat of earth can be most profoundly felt. To attract the attention of gnomes, try playing a drum out in the woods at dusk or at night.

Connecting with the Elements

When seeking connection with the Faery realm and its elusive inhabitants, it is important to keep the perceptive qualities of the mind grounded in the reality of the world around us, in order that we open ourselves to the deeper levels of that reality and not create a substitute illusory reality through excessive, unrooted mental visualization. Imagination is a powerful tool, and when honed, it can become a sense through which the invisible is perceived. Too often, though, it is misused and its strengths turned against the individual's spiritual awakening through too much well-meaning "guidance." It takes more than a quick attunement or fifteen-minute visualization to build a true connection, but the resulting awareness and opening to wisdom is worth the effort and commitment.

By increasing our awareness of the world and the elements around us, we may start to gain the level of perception necessary to connect with the realm of Faery, which is not so far removed from our own. The following contemplations may be performed on a regular basis, and though they can be performed as visualizations if it really isn't possible for you to get to a suitable location (for example, if you are hundreds of miles from the sea), try to do as many as possible in the locations described. If possible, they should be performed over a period of time—preferably a month (or even a year, concentrating on a different exercise each month), in the order as they are written.

Each of the elements has been divided into three qualities: primal, living, and still. These may be compared to the astrological terms used for the division of the elements within the signs of the zodiac—cardinal, mutable, and fixed—but are more transparent in their meaning. Using this system, we can take it to its logical conclusion and connect different natural states of each element with each zodiacal sign, and even extend it to creating a Faery zodiac, which we will look at as a key to personal identification with the elements later on in this section.

FROM LEFT: **air, fire, water, and earth symbols**

Anna Simon performing the contemplation of air
(photo courtesy of Studio Lotus:
www.studiolotus.co.uk)

Contemplations of Air

Primal

Find a comfortable, peaceful place to stand, sit, or lie, with your legs uncrossed and back straight, anywhere outdoors where you will not be disturbed. Close your eyes and focus on your breath. This is our most primal awareness of the element of air. Breathe in deeply, savoring the sensation…breathe out once more. Consider how with each breath you are connecting to your surroundings. Air is one moment external, then internal, and then, transformed, returns to an external state. Consider the plants and trees around you, and how this air has already been a part of them as it becomes a part of you. Continue to breathe deeply and then slowly release. Consider any animals and other people who share your air, and how by sharing breath you are all not only physically but spiritually connected.

If you can, hold an image of the alchemical symbol for air, the upward-pointing yellow triangle with a bar across the point, in your mind. The more you practice this, the easier it will become to hold it for longer. Stay with this process for some time until you feel ready to return to normal breathing. Try to maintain your enhanced awareness in your normal waking state.

Living

Choose a high and open place for this contemplation. On a windy day, stand and face the wind, letting it rush and bluster around you. Close your eyes and focus on sensation. Feel the pressure of the wind on your face, on your skin, and as it blows through your hair. Open your arms wide as though you would embrace it, and feel it sweep away any cobwebs of tiredness or worrying thoughts. As the wind grows and wanes, you may lift and lower your arms, physically linking you to its actions and energy. The more you do this, the more in tune you will become. Is it possible the wind is also responding to your intent? Listen closely to the wind as you feel its power…do you hear any notes, any words? Can you feel any sentient awareness within its actions? Imagine yourself being carried away and swept up by the wind, riding the eddies and currents…feel the exhilaration of freedom inherent in the wild wind. This is the realm of the sylphs. Hold this sensation for as long as you wish, and then bring yourself back to earth by lowering your arms and thanking the wind for your experience.

Still

Choose a peaceful sheltered or indoor space for this contemplation, where the air is still. Sit upright in a comfortable position. Look around you. Air touches and interacts with everything you see, even though it is invisible. It fills all spaces. It is liminal, between all things; when it is still, it is barely detectable, yet all life depends upon it. Close your eyes. See if you can feel the very gentle pressure of air upon your skin. Think of the unknown places that air can reach, and all the places on earth the air that is now with you may have been. Is there an impression of those places remaining? Does air have memory? It permeates so much of the world. Let the stillness and wisdom of air still your mind. Be at peace and at one with the stillness of the air around you. It is in the stillness that inspiration may come… Hold this sensation for as long as you will, and bring the peace and clarity with you into your daily life.

Contemplations of Fire

Primal

Choose a sunny day for this contemplation, either outside in a peaceful location or in a room where you can sit in sunlight. Either sit, stand, or lie comfortably within direct sunlight (avoid looking directly at the sun). Keeping your eyes open at first, consider that before humankind harnessed the power of fire, our only source for heat was the sun. Consider the immense primal power contained in this great star that enables all life on our planet to exist, and how miraculous it is that it is just the right distance and temperature for that life—for *your* life.

Look around you…all you can see, you can see because it is touched by the power of the sun. Look at your hands…see how every line and shadow is defined by the light. Now close your eyes…feel the warmth of the sun on your face. Before there was ever flame on earth, there was this great fire in the sky, the light worshipped by our ancestors as the truly life-giving and all-important source that it is. Consider that if you have spirit, and you acknowledge that living things in the world around you have spirit, how mighty the spirit of such a force must be…and yet it is with you every day, not always acknowledged and noticed but intrinsic to life on earth. Hold this thought, and, keeping your breathing steady, try to picture the upward-pointing red triangle that is the elemental symbol for fire in your mind. Your ability to hold this image will improve with practice. Hold this image and sensation for as long as you wish, and then release and return to your normal state with a heightened awareness of the primal force of the element of fire at work in your life.

Living

This contemplation is best performed outside at night with a fire, or, if that is not possible, you may perform it indoors, preferably with an open fire or a candle. Sit or stand close enough to the flames so that you can feel the intensity of the heat without hurting yourself. Watch the flames leap and flicker as though they are dancing. If you have built this fire, is it possible an elemental has come into being through your will and action? See the fire as being like a life…beautiful and glorious for an allotted time, and then gone from this world.

Feel the heat as it reaches your body, and consider the balance between creation and destruction. The warmth of fire can keep you alive, but it can also destroy, as it is with all the elements. They command our respect. Do you sense life and consciousness in the flames? This is the realm of the salamander, living fire. Listen to all the sounds and watch the shapes of the flames. Does fire have a message for you? Watch until the flames start to die down and the last flickering blue flames remain…watch and listen, scrying into the embers until you are ready to leave the fire. Hold the memory of your experience with you as you return to normal awareness.

Still

This contemplation may be performed indoors or any peaceful outdoor location where you are sheltered and will not be interrupted. Seat yourself comfortably and close your eyes, turning your attention inwards. Place your hands over your solar plexus, your energetic centre. The third expression of the element is your own inner fire. Feel the warmth that is generated by your body. Consider the electrical signals and impulses that are passing through you constantly. These physical aspects are part of your inner fire. It goes much deeper than this. Within each of us is a spark of the Divine. Just as there is a star burning at the centre of our world, so each of us has a spiritual core, a star burning in our centre. Just as the stars above and all existence are connected in a web of energy, so our inner star is connected to all life—to all divine sparks within all living beings.

Feel the power emanating from your core. This is your eternal self that will outlive the body and is connected to all eternity. You do not need to seek for connection…it is already inherent within you. Keep your breathing steady, and feel the power of your will—your ability to act on decision. These things are undeniable, and they are part of the ineffable flame within. Stay with these thoughts and sensations for as long as you are comfortable, then slowly return to normal awareness, bringing the memory and sense of connection back with you into your everyday life.

Contemplations of Water

Primal

For this contemplation it is preferable to be in close physical proximity to the sea. However, this is not possible for many, so it may be performed as a visualization, in which case I recommend finding a good audio recording of ocean waves to listen to.

See the primal vastness of the ocean before you. Watch the waves; feel the rhythm like a heartbeat as they surge forward and then retreat. Listen to the crashing of the waves and feel the power, power that can be harnessed but never tamed. Remember that just as most of your body is water, so it is with the surface of our world. Also remember that the water in your body is affected by the cycles of the moon, just as it is with the tides of the ocean. Set your mind and heart to contemplating that all life first arose from the ocean…she is the first womb, Great Mother of us all, of all creatures…we share this mother, so all forms of life are our brothers and sisters in creation. As you contemplate this, hold in your mind the symbol for water, a simple downward-turned triangle in blue. You realize that this shape reflects the shape of a womb, and that the inner world reflects the outer, and vice versa. Keeping your breath steady as the rhythm of the waves, you may stay with this state as long as you wish, bringing the awareness of connection back with you into your everyday life.

Living

For this contemplation, find a natural spring, stream, or river where you can sit undisturbed for a time. Seat yourself comfortably as near to the running water as you can. Watch the water as it flows through the landscape. Though it seems gentle, its power has worn a path through the land over centuries, smoothing the rocks and soil of mighty

earth. Listen to the sounds of the rushing water as it bubbles and splashes…can you hear song within it? Laughter? This is the living realm of the beauteous undines, the elementals of water.

Has this water come from the realm of above as rain? Has it emerged from a spring from the depths of the underworld? It has been both, and it now carries the memory of above and below. Water flows through us, just as it flows through the world. Again, within and without are mirrors of each other—our connections hidden in plain view. You see and understand how much a part of the world you truly are. Stay with this sensation for as long as you wish, and bring the awareness back with you into everyday life.

Still

For the contemplation of still water, find a small lake or pool in a peaceful location by which you can comfortably sit undisturbed. See the surface of the water. What is reflected on the surface? At the same time, can you see the bottom of the pool through the clear water? Imagine the reflection of the world above as a world in its own right, and that you could dive through the water into the otherworld. Close your eyes and picture this world beneath…a world of truth and memory of all ages. How does this world differ from our own? What beings dwell within? Hold in your mind the thought of all the times and happenings that may have been reflected in these waters, their energy held there still.

With deep and even breath, empty your mind of interrupting thoughts. When your mind is clear, it is like the surface of the water. It may reflect the above and reveal the below. Every unfocused thought is as a stone thrown into the lake, casting ripples about it and distorting the reflection, obscuring what lies beneath. Spend time contemplating the water, its reflections, and what lies below, both in this world and the otherworld. Your mind is like the surface of the water. Stay with this connection for as long as you wish, and bring the understanding back with you into everyday life.

Contemplations of Earth

Primal

For this contemplation, simply find a peaceful outdoor space where you can lie undisturbed on the ground. The primal manifestation of the element of earth is the earth itself, the ground beneath our feet. Lying on the ground, allow yourself to completely relax…trust. Close your eyes and feel how the earth supports you. You could not be more stable than you are now, putting your trust in the earth. Send your awareness down through your body. Imagine you are melding into the earth, all tensions easing away. Let your awareness pass down into the earth beneath you. As it supports you, so it supports all life. Within it lies the fuel for all growth. Be aware of your physical body, your flesh and bones…it too is part of the earth and will become earth when your spirit no longer needs its vessel, just as all your ancestors have passed into earth. You rest upon their wisdom. When you walk, you walk upon their shoulders.

Can you sense the deep, slow heartbeat of earth beneath you? Listen for the heartbeat like a deep, deep drum coming from below. As you do so, see the image of the green inverted triangle (with the bar across the point) that is the symbol for this element. Hold this for as long as you wish, and when you are ready, bring the sense of connection back with you into your daily awareness.

Living

For this contemplation, find some woodland or simply a tree that calls to you in a private location. When you have found a particular tree that you wish to connect with, first stand at a polite distance from the tree. Look at the tree as though you were beholding it for the first time. See how its branches reach up to the light, how strong its trunk is, and picture how deep into the ground the roots grow, mirroring the branches above. Standing before the tree, perform the Faery Tree exercise and see that trees are our closest cousins in the plant world. Know that we must have strong roots in the hidden places in order to have great branches that reach up to the light. Both light and dark in balance are the path to strength in wisdom.

Once this is complete, enter into the energy field of the tree and hold up your hand in greeting. Introduce yourself according to your personal etiquette. Do you feel the tree respond? Can you sense the energy of the tree with your hand? If it feels appropriate to do so, you may sit with your back against the tree and close your eyes, or hold the tree in an embrace. Know that this tree is a living, growing being…the growth is slow and strong, ever reaching higher above and deeper below. Allow your awareness to travel down the trunk of the tree and into the roots. The roots reach down into the unseen lands beneath, untouched by the hands of man. Can you feel the strength of growth reaching down into the hard earth? Will the tree whisper any secrets to you of that land beneath? This is the realm of the gnomes, the elementals of earth. You may also commune with the dryad, the spirit of the tree. Silence can be as much of a gift as words. When you are ready, bring your awareness back up the tree and bring the connection back with you into your daily life.

Still

For this contemplation, you need either a stone that you can hold in your hand or a peaceful place where there are rocks or boulders. Be sure that you will be undisturbed. Make yourself comfortable, with your hands upon the stone. What do you feel? Is the stone warm or cold? Does it seem to respond to your touch? Close your eyes and put your awareness into the stone. Its age is almost unfathomable. Try to imagine what its journey must have been to get to this moment in time. Volcanoes…the Ice Age…what has this stone seen?

Some say that the only living things are those that grow, yet can you not feel that this still stone also has life? Holding the stone and emptying your mind of everyday thought, see what images or sounds arise; will the stone sing to you? It grows warm with your touch as your energies combine. You understand the qualities that led the ancestors to build circles of stone to mark and channel the sacred energies.

When you are ready, withdraw from the stone, but bring your new understanding and sense of connection with you into your everyday life.

The Faery Zodiac

Dividing the four elements into three different qualities, we find ourselves with a direct elemental parallel to the western zodiac system. I have assigned appropriate Faery beings and myths to these twelve elemental divisions to give us a Faery zodiac. Not only is this an interesting way to look at the different beings and stories that are associated with the varied environmental manifestations of the elements, but it is also an excellent way of personally identifying with the qualities of the elements and their spiritual personalities. This is, of course, only a brief look at the sun signs and does not take into account the full complexity of astrology with the positioning of the other planets, but there is certainly scope to take these ideas and develop them further as a system.

March 21–April 20
(Primal Fire—Sol)
LUGH THE WARRIOR

Lugh Lamfada ("long-armed") is a great warrior-poet and champion of the Tuatha de Danann, the gods of ancient Ireland from whom it is said the sidhe are descended. He is also known as Lugh Samildanach, which means "many-skilled," for he was admitted to Tara, the sacred home of the Tuatha, on the grounds that although they had many amongst them who were highly skilled in the same areas as Lugh, there were none like him who were highly skilled in all areas.

People of this sign are natural leaders if they can learn to manage their quick tempers. There may be a tendency to react passionately and rush headfirst into challenging situations without fully thinking it through, but there is also a likelihood that luck will be with them, as well as the skill to come out on top. Warriors are ambitious but noble, channeling their fiery natures into ambitions that benefit those they care about. They are driven by a strong will and can inspire others with their charismatic natures.

April 21–May 20
(Still Earth—Stone)
GOGMAGOG THE GIANT

Gogmagog was a guardian of the ancient land of Kernow, once a country in its own right, now known as Cornwall in the southwest of Britain. Giants are known through the folklore and mythology of many lands around the world for their great size and for being intimately connected with the landscape. Unusual stone formations usually have their stories of great contests between giants or of giantesses who drop stones from their enormous aprons. They are also known for their great appetite!

People of this sign tend to be as reliable as stone itself. Though they may at times be slow to act, when they do, it is decisive and focused and little can get in their way. They are fond of the good things in life, and when they are in happy and stable conditions, they have a giant's appetite! However, when they are unsettled or in stressful circumstances, they can be a force to be reckoned with. A giant in a temper cannot be reasoned with, and other signs may well find themselves giving way to the sheer force of this sign. However, they are generally gregarious, sensual, and loving in relationships.

The Cheesewring, Cornwall

Tamara Newman, "Ocean's Daughter"

(www.tamaranewman.com)

May 21–June 21

(Living Air—Wind)

PEGASUS THE WINGED HORSE

Pegasus, the winged horse and steed of victorious warriors, is one of the most iconic magickal beasts of Greek mythology. Though his mythical origins are of the element of water, being born of Poseidon and Medusa, this beast is clearly associated with the more dynamic qualities of the element of air. Graceful and powerful, Pegasus can be seen as a personification of the wild wind itself.

People of this sign, like Pegasus himself, fly high and fast through life, often leaving others behind them. They are mercurial, and often their speech is as fast and intense as their thoughts. With a tendency to think out loud in rapidly shifting trains of thoughts, they can be fascinating yet exhausting company. Just as Pegasus's fame comes through the deeds of others to whom he was indispensible, so people of this sign display great loyalty and devotion and work well as part of a partnership or team. Because their minds are like the wind itself, never still, they can seem to change their minds often. This is not hypocrisy or a split personality, however, but rather an exploration of all angles in the search for truth.

June 22–July 22

(Primal Water—Ocean)

LIBAN THE MERMAID

Liban was an extraordinary figure, being the offspring of a union between Etain of the Tuatha de Danann and Eochaid of the Firbolg, who was transformed into a mermaid and eventually canonized by the Catholic Church as St. Murgan. Mermaids, beautiful women with the tails of fish, can be found in mythology and folklore all over the world. Quite often they are helpful and friendly to humanity, and in some cases they can even appear as humans when out of water. However, for every tale of a beneficent mermaid there is a darker encounter to recall, often of their haunting song and captivating beauty luring sailors and other unsuspecting souls to their doom.

People of this sign are deeply emotional and sensitive, befitting the association with the element of water in its most primal form. When they fall in love, it becomes their whole world, and their moods can become dark indeed when they are betrayed or disappointed. People of this sign are often natural healers and tend to be driven by compassion for others. They have a love of music and can be talented singers, channeling their emotional natures into creative expression.

July 23–August 22

(Still Fire—Inner Light)

MYRDDIN THE SEER

A key figure of the Faery world both past, mythic, and present is the Faery seer, the most famous of which must be Myrddin Wylt, who later became Merlin, trusted mystic and advisor to King Arthur. Born to a mortal princess and immortal father, Merlin is believed to be either half demon or half faerie, and he certainly is holder of many keys to the mysteries of the otherworld. As one who expresses the power of his inner fire through the gift of prophecy, Myrddin sees what others do not and as such is more occupied by the "bigger picture" of life and by bringing his plans for the greater good to fruition than he is about the individual.

People of this sign may possess great charisma and vision but find it difficult to accept and assimilate the views of others. They often possess great confidence and an awareness of their talents, and this can lead to a clear sense of direction from an early age. The downside of this is a tendency towards the egocentric. They can be intensely charismatic and are excellent communicators, giving them the ability to influence people in their favour. Although they can lead, they tend to do so subtly from the background rather than stepping forward. Though they have no trouble making their ideas understood, their emotions tend to be well controlled, and they will only allow those with whom they are very close to see their true feelings.

August 23–September 22

(Living Earth—Wood)

EURYDICE THE DRYAD

Dryad is word from Greek mythology taken from the Greek word *drys*, which means "oak." Though in the original context they were believed to be the beautiful female spirits of oak trees specifically, it is now used as a general term for most tree spirits. One of the most well-known dryads from ancient myth is Eurydice, the lover of Orpheus. This famous tale tells how the beautiful Eurydice was suddenly killed by a venomous snake that was hidden in the grass. Orpheus valiantly pursues her spirit to the underworld, where he confronts Hades and convinces him to allow her spirit to return, on the condition that as he ascends he does not look behind him to check that she follows him. Tragically, Orpheus cannot help himself, and as he turns to look, Eurydice is lost to him forever.

Just as dryads are closely connected to their tree, so it is that people of this sign have a love of their home and may not be keen on too much travel or adventure. They tend to be shy and reserved, though intelligent and with a great eye for detail. Although they find it difficult to trust others, when trust is won they are loyal and steadfast, and their buried sensuality may flourish with the right person. Dryads love the natural world, and people of this sign make keen gardeners, liking their space to be as perfect as possible.

September 23–October 22
(Primal Air—Breath)
GOBEITHION THE HORN

Through the mythology of the world and in many cultures, there are tales of warriors who sleep in the hollow hills awaiting a time of great need, when they will awaken. In the British Isles this is usually King Arthur and his knights or sometimes Merlin. In a number of versions of this tale, there is a horn that must be blown to awaken the sleeping king and his knights, alongside a sword that must be drawn. The power of the horn to wake those who have been lost to enchanted sleep for so many centuries is testament to the primal power of the element of air through our own breath. The name given to this sign of the Faery zodiac is Gobeithion, which is the Welsh word for "hopes." This seems fitting, as the horn that wakes the sleepers carries the hopes of the land in its music.

People of this sign have a naturally noble nature that can be taken incorrectly for snobbery. They have an awareness of their calling in life and are concerned with justice and maintaining harmony. This can mean that they seem emotionally detached, but in reality they prefer to be objective in order to be fair to everyone, as they care so deeply about the rights of others. Truth is highly important to them, yet they are sensitive to the fact that truth can be personal and subjective, so are sometimes easily swayed. Gobeithion people may be crusaders for just causes, but usually from behind the scenes rather than as figureheads. They have a keen aesthetic sense and enjoy creative expression, particularly in the field of music.

October 23– November 22

(Still Water—Lakes and Ponds)

NIMUE, THE LADY OF THE LAKE

Lakes have long been acknowledged as gateways to the otherworld and the magickal dwellings of Faery women. There are many tales of lake maidens who are the custodians of otherworldly wisdom and, at the same time, the breakers of men's hearts. One of the more well-known of these maidens is the Lady of the Lake of Arthurian fame, who gifts Excalibur to the young King Arthur and is the lover of the great seer and sorcerer Merlin. Most known versions of this tale tell how she seduced and betrayed Merlin, trapping him in a tree or a hole beneath a stone, but these are late additions. Her origins lie in an ancient sister and lover of Merlin's who was in every way his equal, a priestess to his priest, the intuitive and receptive female polarity of magick.

Just like a lake, what is happening on the surface of this sign may not always show what lies beneath. They are good at keeping secrets and have a natural awareness of the mysteries of life. They are naturally intuitive and creative but may at times use their intuition to manipulate others. Generally they prefer to keep people at a safe distance, but when they do allow people to become close, as they will with a select few, they are deeply intense. There are two sides to everyone, but this is particularly apparent in Nimue people, as beneath the sparkling, seductive surface, there is a dark side that, fed by a fertile imagination, can be sensual and erotic but also sensitive, with a tendency to hold on to painful memories.

November 23–December 21

(Living Fire)

LADON THE DRAGON

Ladon was the great twisting serpentlike dragon who guarded the famous golden apples in the Garden of the Hesperides in Greek mythology. Apples are a symbol of wisdom, so we can see this as the dragon being a guardian of ancient wisdom. In world mythology, dragons take many forms and have varying powers and qualities. They have been seen as both malevolent and beneficent, but they are almost always guardians of some kind, either of treasure or of a sacred place. Often the defeating of a dragon challenger is a form of initiation for mythic heroes, allowing them access to the wisdom that was so carefully guarded until he was ready.

People born under the sign of Ladon the Dragon can be as difficult to pin down as the great serpent himself! They often have many interests and facets and pursue them all with great vigor. People of this sign have their own treasure to guard, however, so whilst many things about their lives will often shift and change, the things that are precious to them will be a well-protected constant. This may well be their spiritual beliefs, which are often important to Ladon people, to whom tradition and ritual are of high importance. This sign also enjoys challenging others, as they like to see what makes people tick. Just like a dragon, if you can pass their tests, you may be admitted to the treasure of their wisdom.

December 22–January 20

(*Primal Earth*)

PAN THE FAUN

Pan is an ancient god of Greek origin, thought to predate the Olympian gods. The Greeks worshipped him as a god of pastures and flocks, and his goatlike form as a faun reflected this association. In modern practice it is generally accepted that Pan is a primal force, the male polarity of nature itself and the rhythm of life. He was famous for his pursuit of passionate exchanges with nymphs of the forest, and also for the sweet music played on his pipes. He is the lord of beasts and the spirit of the wild, sharing many qualities of other horned gods such as the Celtic Cernunnos and the more recent Herne the Hunter of British folklore.

The earthy nature of this sign makes it highly practical in nature. People of this sign like to see results and rewards for their endeavors and can be very driven by material reward. When they are focused on a task they can be relentless if they can see the potential gain from it, but if not they can become uninterested and disheartened. When this happens, Pan people can rapidly fall into very dark moods, but if their needs are met they can be lifted out of the darkness just as rapidly. They have a need to be secure and stable in a relationship and are very loyal if they meet the right person.

January 21–February 19

(Still Air—The Space Between)

LEANAN SIDHE THE MUSE

Leanan Sidhe ("Faery lover") is a Faery muse of Irish origin said to visit artists and poets and bring them otherworldly inspiration. However, this gift is said to shorten the life of the gifted individual, as if the inspiration of the muse somehow uses up their life force. This can been seen as a malignant act on the part of the Leanan Sidhe, but from another perspective the poet gives up his earthly life to be with his Faery lover. This is most likely a form of Faery pact, with the poet producing beautiful work for a while in his earthly life, and then being taken to the otherworld to dwell with the sidhe.

People of this sign are gifted visionaries who seem to have an inexhaustible well of inspiration at their disposal, as well as the gift to inspire others. However, the constant activity of their minds can exhaust them, and they will often need time and space away from others to recharge their batteries. They can be entertaining in a group, if baffling and eccentric at times, but Leanan Sidhe people only let a few become close and see their true character. Whether through science, religion, or a combination of the two, people of this sign are most concerned with finding a universal truth and with expressing the beauty of truth to the world.

February 20–March 20

(Living Water—Rivers and Streams)

ONDINE THE NYMPH

Ondine was a beautiful nymph from a French tale of love, magick, and loss. She fell in love and married a mortal man, giving up her immortal life and beauty. He swears on his breath that he will be loyal to her forever, but once she bears his child, her looks begin to fade, and he soon betrays her. She finds him sleeping in the arms of another and curses him that if he should ever fall asleep again, he will lose the breath that he swore by. Nymphs are beautiful female spirits of water and are purely emotional creatures. This emotion becomes vengefully and lethally motivated when they are given cause.

People of this sign are highly emotional and intuitive individuals. They are extremely generous with their energy; they love to please others and make them happy, often sacrificing their own happiness and even health to do so. As long as people are appreciative of them, they do not begrudge their sacrifices, though they may have slightly martyred tendencies. However, if they are disappointed in the subject of their emotional invest-ment, they are quick to revenge. They are natural healers and are highly empathic, but they have little control over their empathy, so they often get the emotions of others confused with their own. Ondine people find most happiness through the happiness of others, finding it difficult to pursue their own needs and ambitions. They can be highly creative, as they have wonderful imaginations, but this is also something that is often sacrificed for others.

EXERCISE: Faery Zodiac

Consider which sign you fall under within the Faery zodiac and how your personality is reflected in the elemental qualities of that sign. You may wish to do further research into the stories behind your sign, and make notes of any personal significance. If you know your time and place of birth, you can easily get a full birthchart drawn up; there are many free programs online that can do this for you. Consider where your elemental strengths and weaknesses lie, and how you may seek to find elemental balance through your alliances with the Faery realm. Look at the influence of the planets and consider how they have manifested so far in your life. What does this information tell you about the challenges you face in this life? What gifts do you manifest and what still lies latent and in potential? How can you uncover and develop this potential? What lessons are you here to learn? These are all questions that are worth exploring with the aid of your Faery allies.

Suggested Activities

Practice

Take time over the course of a month to perform each of the elemental contempla-tions in turn, doing as many of them as possible (preferably all) in appropriate outdoor locations. Do not rush by trying to do them all in one day, but you may choose to do more than one if the time you are able to spend in an appropriate location is limited. Remember to makes notes of your experiences, however subtle they may be.

Consider your Faery zodiac sign as suggested in the above exercise. If you are artistic, you may choose to create an image of this sign or of yourself as the elemental being. Alternatively, build a mental picture in your imagination.

Daily Routine

Try to find a few minutes during your day—either first thing in the morning or last thing at night would be best—to build a daily practice, incorporating the Becoming the Faery Tree exercise and any other of the exercises so far that you have found effective (for instance, Voice Work). Since voice work uses physical muscles and is deeply connected to your personal energy, the more you practice, the stronger it will become. You may choose to use your previously created Faery symbol centrepiece as a focus for this work.

Create

Once you have completed all the elemental contemplations at least once, consider what understanding you have gained of each element and apply them to the following creative tasks. Remember these are for you and your Faery allies, not for an outside audience, so do not allow fear of judgement to block your raw creativity.

* Write a poem or song about your experience of the element of air.

* Devise and perform a dance that expresses your experience of the element of fire (according to your physical capacity—even just hand movements can carry much energy and expression).

* Using modelling clay, create a piece that expresses something of your understanding and experience of the element of earth. It may be as abstract or representative as you choose.

* Paint an image in watercolours that expresses something of your experience understanding the element of water, as abstract or representative as you wish.

CHAPTER THREE
Trust

"Trust dreams, trust your heart, and trust your story…"

Neil Gaiman, *Instructions*

• • • • • • •

Chapter 3 is dedicated to the direction of north, the element of earth, and the quality of trust. In this chapter we will explore such themes as the land of Faery, the underworld journey, and finding a Faery ally. We will also look at the sacred landscape and learn about locations where our world and the otherworld interact, leading to a powerful exercise called Walking in Awareness.

At first glance you may wonder why this chapter is called "trust," but in fact it is at this stage that trust becomes a vital quality in order to progress in Faery Craft. By this point you have built a foundation of knowledge and started to develop awareness of and connection with the land around you. In order to deepen your relationship with Faery and form bonds with sacred places, guardians, and Faery allies, you will need to be able to trust. It is usual at this stage to have lots of questions, the most common being "How do I know that what I am experiencing isn't just in my imagination?" Questioning is an important process, and it is important not to blindly accept everything (remember, you can ask questions of your Faery allies when you start journeying and communicating with them). At the same time, it is possible to get caught up in unconstructive circular questioning that can only be escaped with the aid of trust.

Trust the work that you have done so far, trust your inner guides and allies, and, above all, learn to let go and trust yourself. The exercises and activities so far should have prepared you for taking your journey a step further, and as long as you stay grounded and true to yourself, the path will unfold before you…

The Land of Faery

*"Sometimes lying on the hillside with the eyes of the body shut
as in sleep I could see valleys and hills, lustrous as a jewel,
where all was self-shining, the colours brighter and purer,
yet making a softer harmony together than the colours of the
world I know. The winds sparkled as they blew hither and
thither, yet far distances were clear through that glowing air."*

AE, A *Candle of Vision*

• • • • • • •

Although we may encounter Faery beings in our realm when they choose to appear or in locations and times where the veil between our worlds is thinnest, the world that they inhabit has many differences from our own. It is also intimately linked with our world, and, though separate, is the same. Confused? Seeming contradictions such as this are part of the fascinating enigmatic riddle that is Faery.

Time and form work differently in the Faery realm—indeed, the whole realm is more fluid and less seemingly fixed than our physical world. It is the primal underworld, a place of restoration and renewal, untouched by time and the onslaughts of humanity and yet so interconnected with our world that our changes are keenly felt by them. Just as the seeming appearance of Faery beings changes through our own perceptions, so it is with their land, yet it makes it no less real. As our understanding of the nature of energy grows, so it may be that our perceptions grow closer to the truth, or at least closer to their own. You may find it helpful to consider the Faery realm as something akin to the original DNA of our world, containing the unspoiled blueprint of life, which may be used to restore what has been lost and damaged in our own realm. This is an interesting image when you consider that the road to the underworld is a spiral stair.

The Underworld Journey

As it is so difficult to describe the wonders of the land of Faery, I encourage you to visit yourself. There are many ways by which one might experience the land of Faery, all of which involve entering altered states of consciousness. The following method can be used by anyone, with no need for mind-altering drugs or plants, though in some cases it may take more than one attempt before results are achieved. For this technique you will need either a drum such as a bodhran, which gives a resonant beat, and someone to drum for you, or a recording of a steady drumbeat. These may be found quite readily and are used for shamanic journeying. You may find that you can journey well enough in silence or that you prefer another sound such as running water, ocean waves, the human voice, a musical instrument, or a rattle. This can only be discovered through experience and experimentation.

You will also need a place that you are familiar with in the physical realm that can act as a gateway to Faery. I strongly advise that this be a tree with a natural opening that you can visualize passing through and down into the roots, but other possibilities include a well, a gap in a hedge, or a cave. You do not need to be physically there when you are journeying (though if you are able and would not be disturbed there, it would enhance the experience), but you do need to have been there and be able to re-create it in your mind in strong sensory detail; i.e., sight, smell, touch, and sounds. If your visual imagination is not strong, concentrate on those senses that work best for you.

The following exercise is not a guided visualization, meditation, or pathworking. It is the foundation technique for sending your consciousness into other realms and can be adapted to many different intents and purposes. The most important first task when beginning to explore the inner landscape is to find guides and allies, so this is the intent for the following journey. These allies may take animal, human, or faerie form, and eventually you will gain a group of allies who will have different strengths and specialities, just as you do, that complement each other. They can then aid you in your further purposes, which must not be trivial or materialistic in motive. For example, once you have a guide or ally, you can ask them for assistance in leading you to places of learning to find inner teachers, further guides, or symbols for protection and empowerment.

It is often neglected and extremely important to realize that your guides are beings in their own right and not extensions of your psychology. As such, remember to ask on

Emily Carding, "The Invitation"

your journeys whether there are tasks in this world or theirs with which they require *your* assistance. This is the method by which strong partnerships and enduring friendships are formed.

EXERCISE: *Underworld Journey to Find a Guide*

Make yourself comfortable in a place where you are absolutely sure you will not be disturbed. If you are unused to journeying, it is a good idea to find a space in your home or another secure indoor location where you can lie on the floor with uncluttered space around you. If the room is bright, use a scarf or something similar to cover your eyes. If you have someone to drum for you, be sure they know to keep a slow, regular beat, or find a good shamanic drumming track that you can play on headphones. Remember, you are listening for the sound *between* the beats; this resonant frequency will start to sound almost like song, forming a continuous note that aids in entering a trance state. Before you begin, arrange a callback signal with your drummer, such as three sets of three long beats followed by rapid drumming. Use this signal as an anchor or cord that guides you back to physical reality. Most drum tracks will have this, and you should allow about twenty minutes for your journey.

Take deep breaths and listen to the sound between the drumbeats. Allow it to transport you out of normal awareness. Feel the tension slipping from your body as if you are melting into the earth. Before you, you see the tree or other real-world location that you have chosen as your entry point into the underworld. Build as strong a picture as you can of this place—the colours, the textures, the sounds, and the smells. Do not worry if in our world the entrance is too small for you to pass through; normal rules no longer apply. Either the entrance will grow, or you will shrink. It is possible that you may be met by a guardian at this point, or you may not. Allow for what naturally occurs, and remember to ask questions and not follow blindly or be discourteous. This is not fantasy or role-play; consider how you would act in real life. When you are ready, pass through the entrance.

Before you lies an ancient spiral staircase lit dimly by torchlight. It is spiraling downwards through the earth. Feel the walls; feel the stone beneath your feet. Is there any dampness or moss, or is it dry? Travel down the spiral stairs, deep down into the roots of the tree. Take your time, travelling slowly down the spiral stairs.

The stairs start to brighten, and eventually you emerge into a large cavern of reddish clay. The cavern seems to emit its own light. From above, you can see the roots of a great tree have pushed through the earth and are growing all around you. There are several passageways leading off from the cavern. There may be symbols above these entrances or there may not be. If there are, try to remember them, and make note of them when you return. Before you, sitting in the roots of the tree, is a large being who seems to be part man and part beast. He sits calmly, waiting for you to approach. If he addresses you first, state your business politely and firmly. You tell the figure that you are here to find a guide to the otherworld to help you with your journeys and your work with the Faery realm. He may or may not have more questions, which should all be answered truthfully and politely.

The guardian beats a staff upon the ground, and potential guides of many forms appear—some of which you may recognize, others that you may not, and yet others that seem to continually shift shape. Perhaps it will be only one who enters the chamber. If any seem to act aggressively or are clearly uninterested, they are not your guide. One or more may approach you. Always greet them and ask if they are your guide or if they have another purpose or perhaps a message for you. It is also possible that you will find a power animal or teacher at this point.

Once you have found a guide or power animal, it is best not to attempt to achieve more on a first journey unless they have something important to show you. Ask them to return with you.

Together you travel back up the spiral stairs. Eventually you re-emerge at your original starting point. Either wait here and converse with your guide until the call-back signal or cross your arms across your chest as a signal to your drummer that you are ready to return.

When you are ready, open your eyes and make notes immediately, as some details that may be important later can fade with time. Be slow and careful getting up, and have a glass of water and a small bite to eat or rub your hands with salt to ground yourself.

Maintaining the Relationship with Your Allies

Now that you have formed a link with an otherworldly being, it is important to maintain it, just as you would with any friendship. You can use the basic formula of the journey above to meet with your guide or ally, and if you inform them of your intent, they can help you to find your way in the otherworld, perform tasks, learn, and find more allies. Some will be with you for life, others only for a limited time, for specific tasks. Some will be limited geographically to certain locations; others may be able to travel with you wherever you go. Over time, if you journey regularly, you will build many alliances. You do not need to be in a journey to call upon them; they are with you all the time. Whenever you need strength and support, call on your allies. Remember that in return, they can call on you. Trust them, and never take them for granted.

The Sacred Landscape

"This is a faery stream we're passing; there were some used to see them by the side of it, and washing themselves in it. And there used to be heard a faery forge here every night…"

Lady Gregory, Visions and Beliefs in the West of Ireland

· · · · · · ·

Although the imagination is a valuable tool of perception when properly trained with experience, our first point of contact with the Faery realm must always be in the landscape around us, not in our heads. Too much meditation or journey work without a connection with the land can lead to a difficulty in sensing what is genuine contact and what is illusory. This is why it is important that you are experienced in performing the contemplations of the elements outside in the landscape as featured in chapter 2, Connection, before you progress to deeper journey work such as the Underworld Journey.

Regular contact with nature not only enhances our link with the Faery realm and our ability to sense Faery beings, but it also helps to keep us grounded in our bodies and aware of the physical world around us. We don't necessarily need to live near obviously marked sacred sites to find points in the landscape where our realms overlap; in fact, the most powerful place for you will be the site where you find yourself undisturbed by the footsteps of well-meaning spiritual tourists.

Trees
Trees are our closest spiritual relatives in the plant kingdom, with their roots reaching into the underworld and their branches like arms reaching towards the sun. As such, they are an excellent first point of contact with the inner spiritual landscape and its

inhabitants. Many trees have a strong individual spiritual presence. Others have something more like a hive consciousness, and others can act simply as a window or bridge into another reality. The latter are often hollow trees or trees that have an obvious opening in the roots through which our energy bodies can travel into the underworld. Trees such as oaks, which have a very strong individual presence, can often be home to dryads, who can be useful allies in the Faery realm if they are willing to work with you. Like people, they have distinctive personalities and even moods (though their moods are far slower to change than humans, of course). You must bear this in mind when trying to make contact with the spirit of a tree, for if it is hostile, it is best to leave it alone and find a contact that is more amenable. When first opening your sense to energy, it can sometimes be difficult to differentiate between positive and negative signals. This is something that will come with practice as you hone your intuition and ability to interpret the signal that you are receiving. Again, contact with trees is an excellent place to start!

First Contact

When you have found a tree that you feel drawn to make contact with (for trees particularly associated with Faery, see chapter 5's section on tools), try not to make the mistake of blundering in without properly introducing yourself. Would you go up to a stranger on the street and hug them? Probably not, and if you did, it would most likely result in total bafflement at best.

To begin, stand a short distance from the tree and take in every detail that you can, using all your senses. Breathe deeply and slowly, remembering that the tree inhabits a very different rhythm of life but is no less alive than you are. Mentally acknowledge the individual physical and energetic signature of the tree, and open up your own energy to make a tentative first connection by opening your arms, palms open and facing out. If you feel that it is appropriate, approach the tree slowly with one hand outstretched. With the palm open, see if you can sense the energy field of the tree as you approach, stopping either when you feel the edge of the energy field or when you have an impulse to do so. If you are not used to sensing energy and are unsure what to be looking out for, it may manifest as a temperature change or a tingling sensation or even an unusual sensation elsewhere in the body. If at this point you feel the tree does not wish to make contact, it is best to politely withdraw. If, however, you feel welcome to proceed, you may greet the tree and move on to touch the bark of the trunk.

If you are unsure how to greet the tree, this may simply be an energetic exchange or you may choose to sing a short phrase or note. I use a simple salute in which I touch my lips, heart, and forehead and then present my hand outwards in a giving gesture. This represents the devotion, truth, and union of words, thoughts, and deeds, and I also use it to greet sacred sites. Now it is time to close your eyes and allow the energy to flow between yourself and the tree. Images, sensations, and sounds or simply a feeling of peace may come. You are likely to have different experiences with different trees. If the tree is willing, send your awareness into its roots and then into its branches. Try to gain a sense of the tree as a living and aware being. When you have spent the time that you both need for this contact, which you should feel naturally, withdraw gently and give your farewells. If you have had a positive experience, your link will strengthen with repeated visits and you may well forge a valuable inner world contact. This can be further sealed with appropriate offerings and journey work.

Natural Gateways

Gateways are portals found within nature where it is possible to pass through from this worldly awareness into otherwordly awareness. They are an excellent place to begin a walking meditation such as the Walking in Awareness exercise at the end of this chapter. The most common gateways found in nature are when two powerful trees grow together and their branches link overhead. There is a strong energetic presence when this happens, and you may sense or even see a distortion in the air between them. This most commonly occurs with trees most strongly linked to the Faery realm (as you will see listed in the tools section of chapter 5).

Exceptionally powerful gateways may be found when natural arches or holes azre formed from stone, such as in St. Nectan's Glen in Cornwall or Arch Rock on Mackinac Island, Michigan. Caves are obvious gateways into the otherworld and the perfect place to contact and experience earth elementals and underworld beings. Other gateways may be found simply in a gap between hedges or stones. To acknowledge the gateway and experience the shift in awareness, move forward with awareness and stand between the two trees (or whatever is forming the gateway) with your arms reaching to either side, palms outwards. Breathe, close your eyes, and simply experience. When it is not possible to stand in the gateway, you will still find the area around the site to be magickally charged and a good place for connection.

TOP: **St. Nectan's Glen in Cornwall**
LEFT: **Arch Rock on Mackinac Island, Michigan**

Rivers

Water flows through the landscape in rivers and streams just as it carries blood cells around our body in arteries and veins. It is an intrinsically magickal substance and brings an enchanted quality to any area it flows through. Although rivers may not be seen as gateways in the landscape as such, by allowing yourself to relax and simply listen to the natural music of the water, worries can be eased away, and it becomes easier to enter an altered state in which connection and communication can be achieved.

Rivers are often home to water elementals and also attract various Faery beings, as well as possessing their own spirit and identity. The spirit of a river can be a powerful ally for healing work, as you can, with repeated and extended physical contact with its energies, learn to "plug in" to its cleansing energies. This is particularly helpful with ailments caused by energy blockages.

To greet the spirit of a river, open your heart to the flow of energy, and listen intently to the sound of the water. Allow music to rise up within you, and let your song join the sound of the water, linking your energies.

Lakes and Ponds

Naturally formed lakes and ponds are clear gateways to the otherworld, with many having their own ancient folklore attached to them, such as Dozmary Pool in Cornwall, England, which was said to be the home of the Lady of the Lake. There are many tales of faery queens and ladies whose realm is beneath the surface of a great lake, and, as in many of the old stories, there is a magickal truth hidden within. Lakes and ponds of still water are nature's magick mirrors, full of memory and mystery. If you are able to visit a lake during a full moon, when the moon is reflected in the water, this can be a particularly potent time to experience otherworldly energies.

Wells and Springs

Wells and springs, where the waters of the primal underworld emerge into our own surface realm, are extremely important in Faery Craft. They are sources of purity and healing and are usually under the guardianship of at least one Faery being, sometimes in partnership with an elemental. Both site and being/s should always be treated with the utmost respect; given time and attention, they can become powerful allies.

It would be wise to discover if you have a well or spring within reasonable travelling distance of your home, as this would be an excellent source of water for any magickal work you wish to perform, including consecrations and purifying space. Find your own way of greeting the well and its guardian/s, perhaps including a phrase, song, and a physical gesture of peace and honour such as the triple salute as mentioned in the previous section on trees. Offerings that leave no debris are also appropriate, but nothing should be placed actually in the waters themselves unless there is a justified long-standing tradition of doing so specific to that site. There are many wells and springs that have established connections with ancient Faery lore and myth, but in truth they are all connected and all sacred. All wells are one well, and when your awareness and sense of connection grows, you will start to feel the power that is held by their network of energies and the powerful link to the renewing energies of the underworld.

TOP: Dozmary Pool, Cornwall
LEFT: St. Torney's Well, Cornwall

Hills

The Faery nobility are said to dwell within the hollow hills, and there are many examples throughout the world of high places where the power of the spirit of the land can be felt. Throughout folklore there are tales of people being taken into Faery through entrances in hills, often relating to genuine cases of real disappearances or mysterious deaths. One of the most famous of these hills is Doon Hill in Aberfoyle, Scotland, which is where it is said the Reverend Robert Kirk, author of *The Secret Commonwealth of Elves, Fauns, and Faeries,* was taken into Faery to become a mediator between the worlds. Another famous example of a Faery hill is Glastonbury Tor in Somerset, England, beneath which it is said dwells Gwyn Ap Nudd, the Faery king.

Ancient hill forts also are particularly powerful locations for contact with Faery and the ancestors. Not all places of power have such established folklore associated with them, but they often seem to stand out from the landscape and can easily be spotted. Faery hills radiate a certain charisma that is difficult to explain but is readily felt, in the same way that charismatic people stand out from the crowd. Often sites of ancient power may have hill forts or churches built upon them, as people throughout history have been drawn by their natural magnetism.

To connect with the spirit of a hill, spend time in stillness and contemplation, preferably at the top of the hill or within close proximity. The experience will most likely vary according to each hill's history and nature, so allow your intuition and allies to guide you.

Stone Circles

It is difficult to say whether the ancients used the thousands of stone circles, henges, monoliths, and avenues across the landscape of Britain and Europe as ways of honouring preexisting sacred spaces or intentionally created them as places of power, but what is certain is that they stand today as places between the worlds where the veil is thin and the power of the land can be keenly felt.

When approaching a stone circle or henge, it is appropriate to seek out the gateway, or guardian stones of the circle, and greet them before entering. It will normally be obvious which these are, but if it is not, walk around the outside of the circle in a clockwise direction and see if you feel drawn to enter in a particular place, then greet the two stones that create that entrance. To sit with your back against an ancient stone under a starlit sky is to touch the magick of the Old Ones.

TOP: Chalice Well
RIGHT: Glastonbury Tor (both in Glastonbury)

Chalk Figures and White Horses

In the chalk downs of Southern England there are a large number of chalk figures carved into the landscape. These are mostly of white horses, which were sacred to the ancient Celts and Britons as symbols of sovereignty and were associated with a number of gods and goddesses as well as with Faery. There are also giants such as the Cerne Abbas giant in Somerset, which is said to mark the final resting place of a real giant and is still to this day visited by couples seeking to enhance their fertility. There is also the Long Man of Wilmington, who appears to be holding two staves but could also be holding open a doorway into the hill.

Neil Gaiman graphically followed this line of thought in his wonderful Sandman graphic novels, showing Queen Titania, King Oberon, and the Faery host emerging from the hill through the Long Man's gateway to enjoy the first-ever production of Shakespeare's A *Midsummer Night's Dream*.

Hedgerows

By their very nature, hedgerows are spaces that define the liminal. Ancient border markers that teem with abundant flora and fauna, hedgerows are rich in Faery lore and are obvious places to feel the presence of nature spirits and Faery beings. Be wary, though, as many of the beings associated with the hedgerow are as dark and prickly as the thorn bushes themselves, so be sure to always greet them with respect and keep your wits about you. Time spent in stillness near a hedgerow will start to reveal its secrets, and you may find that you start to notice faces and other features within the branches, leaves, and roots. Listen to the whispers of the wind through the leaves. See if they have a message for you, and be ready to answer a riddle!

Burial Mounds

The connection between the Faery race and the resting places of the dead is so intimate that in Scotland and Ireland they were even called by the same name: sidhe. Burial mounds are intentionally constructed to be gateways into the underworld; as such, they are powerfully liminal spaces for Faery contact. Many such ancient sites were aligned with the cycles of the sun, moon, and stars, such as Newgrange in Ireland, where the entrance is aligned with the midwinter dawn; this adds to their significance as points

Native American Burial Chamber,
Mackinac Island, Michigan

of contact for Faery Craft. However, it must be remembered that burial mounds are also the resting places of the ancestors, and they must always be honoured alongside the sidhe when you are working in their space.

When approaching a burial mound, keep respectful silence. The triple salute mentioned earlier is an appropriate greeting, and offerings of beer and wine are usually welcomed, but be sure not to leave any mess behind you.

Mountains

Mountains are powerful forces of liminality, reaching from the depths of the underworld to the heady realms of the cosmos. They are sacred places in many cultures
throughout the world, often formed by the stone-throwing contests of giants or from
the sleeping forms of giants themselves. Mountains are the perfect place to experience
the awesome power of nature and the spirit within the land, having been formed by
primal forces and enduring many ages.

Due to the size and slow (compared to us) energetic heartbeat of the great mountain
spirits, they are often unaware of humans. However, there will most likely be several
or even a huge number of spirits of place within and around a mountain. There will be
the spirit of the mountain itself, possibly a faery queen and/or king, and quite possibly
a whole kingdom and hierarchy beneath them. Address the spirits of the mountain as if
you were a visitor at a noble court.

The Hurlers, Cornwall

Other Sites

Not all places where the worlds meet are so obviously marked. Certain fields may be full of Faery activity, as may any space where there is growth or the potential for growth. In fact, Faery encounters can happen in such unexpected places as airports, train stations, and busy streets. Just because it is a built-up area in our reality doesn't mean that there are not still places where the worlds overlap. However, the busy world of humanity, with its confusing electrical and airborne signals, is not conducive to the peace and harmony required for enduring Faery contact, which is best found in the green places of the earth.

Flowers and Fungi

Certain flowers have strong associations with Faery, such as bluebells, snowdrops, red campion, foxgloves, and roses, to name only a few. As is well noted in folklore, rings of mushrooms or toadstools, particularly the highly toxic and hallucinogenic fly agaric, are known as fairy rings. It is said that these are places where the people of Faery dance on starlit nights. It is also said that if you enter the dance, you may be taken into Faery and not return for many centuries, so such sites must be treated with great caution.

Timing

Although contact may be made either spontaneously or intentionally at any time (expect the unexpected when dealing with the Faery realms!), there are times of the day, month, and year when the connection between worlds is strongest and you are more likely to feel their presence. Dusk and dawn are powerful times to be out in nature. There are often fewer people around, and there is a tangible sense of magick in the air as you are between the night and the day. Around the hour of midnight is also a potent time; however, do take care that you don't pass into places where you are not welcome or that are dangerous for more mortal reasons. The full moon is the best time for blessings, consecrations, and leaving offerings for Faery, whereas the new moon is best for divination and channelling work.

During the course of the year there are times when the worlds are considered to be closer together, when the veil between them is thinner. The days that are most associated with Faery are Beltane, which in the Northern Hemisphere is celebrated between April 31 and May 2 (or, if you prefer a more natural method, when the hawthorn starts flowering), Midsummer (June 21/22), and Samhain (October 31). If you are in the Southern Hemisphere, Midsummer and Midwinter (or, if you prefer, the Summer and Winter Solstices) are swapped round, as are the dates for Beltane and Samhain.

Far more important than the dates and traditions of cultures that might not necessarily relate directly to you is paying attention to the cycles of nature around and within you. Watch for when certain plants are flowering and fading. Pay attention to the cycles of the moon. Be aware of changes in the weather. Feel for the shifts in energy around you. When life is returning to the land, or fading back into the otherworld, these are the times when the presence of Faery can be most keenly felt.

Guardians

All sacred sites and places of power will have their guardians, and they must be treated with great respect. When greeting a site, you should consider finding your own way to acknowledge the power and importance of the place, honour the guardians, and introduce yourself. Show that you come with pure intent and integrity and that you mean no harm to the spirit of place or to the land itself. These are things that may be shown through energy and action in harmony, and any impurity of energy will be sensed easily by Faery beings. Any attempt to deceive them or to simply feed the human ego through your magickal endeavours will result in a descent into illusion and loss of true connection.

Guardians may take many forms, both energetic and physical. Energetic forms vary wildly in appearance, nature, and size, according to the nature of the site. Your ability to sense their nature will improve with the amount of time spent building connection with the land and Faery. They will usually display an inclination towards the elemental strength of that area—for example, white ladies at water sites, giants at mountains, dryads in forests, and so on. Guardians often take the physical form of wild creatures, so be very aware of the behaviour of any animals you encounter when visiting places of power. For example, once when collecting water with a friend and fellow priestess for a ritual from an ancient pool, one of a crowd of wild ponies on the site left the others and walked some distance to stand directly in the path in front of us, blocking our way. We all stood there for some time until it occurred to me to ask politely if we may take the water from their pool, at which point it nodded agreement and rejoined the other ponies.

You can see a most dramatic example of wild creatures acting as guardians in some film footage that was captured at a protest site in Newbury, UK, in the late 1990s. As ancient oaks are felled, two wild black horses seem to come from nowhere and start to confront the workmen, the police, and, in a most moving moment, the police horses. If you search for "wild horses of Newbury" on YouTube, you can watch this extraordinary footage for yourself.

At other times guardians may be as small as a garden robin, but they are no less powerful and should never be disregarded. Awareness of the world around you and its intimate link with Faery is key.

Finding Your Power Place

Even in an urban environment it is possible to find a location or several locations that resonate with your energy, enabling you to establish a profound link to the inner landscape. The Walking in Awareness exercise at the end of this chapter is a useful technique to find the areas in your landscape that you are energetically drawn to. Spend as much time as you can outdoors without distractions, keeping the mobile phone and portable

Wild horses near standing stones

music player switched off. Be open to all sensory input, see where time and again you feel most drawn to, most energized, or most at peace. It could be a particular tree in a city park, a spot in the garden, or an overgrown patch of land.

If you can find somewhere that you will be able to spend time undisturbed, this can become a power place for you, a place where you make strong connections with the guardians and spirits of place and are renewed by the primal energy of the inner landscape. This connection can be built through offerings and meditation, as well as the exercises and suggestions in this book.

Dowsing

You may wish to use dowsing techniques to aid you in building an energetic map of your area and help you to find places of power in the land. Simple tools such as a pendulum or dowsing rods can be used very effectively for this purpose, or if you are naturally energy sensitive, you may find that with your palms open and receptive, you are able to feel physical sensations such as changes in temperature and tingles, almost like static electricity, when beings or places of power are near. The more you practice this, the more attuned this sense (or extension of the senses) will become, and the more detail you will start to receive. Don't try *too* hard—this can result in the mind creating illusory results. Instead, take your time, be patient, and allow yourself to feel the authentic energetic nature of the landscape.

Energy Lines

Energy flows across our landscape in interconnected currents, sometimes known as dragon lines or ley lines. Consider this matrix of energy to be something like the nervous system of our planet. Like rivers, these currents of energy may change their course over time and be affected by activity in their surroundings, such as roads, power lines, mobile phone signals, and construction. If sites such as stone circles were created to harness these energy currents, it is worth considering whether in some cases the lines may have changed their course. In any case, there is an ever-shifting landscape of energies laid out in front of you, full of places of power that are yet to be discovered.

The Walking in Awareness Exercise

*"It's a dangerous business, Frodo, going out of your door," he
used to say. "You step into the Road, and if you don't keep your
feet, there is no knowing where you might be swept off to…"*

J. R. R. Tolkien, *The Lord of the Rings*

· · · · · · ·

This exercise begins as an extended version of the Faery Tree exercise, and it will benefit
your level of awareness to practice the first stage a number of times before you expand
it further into the walking meditation. The purpose of this exercise is threefold. It will
enhance your general level of awareness and attention to detail, it will increase your
sensitivity to energy, and it will enable to you locate your places of power within the
landscape as well as potential tools and allies, depending on the intent with which you
set off.

Many years ago I performed a similar exercise, and it was one of the most profound
experiences of my life, which is why I suggest it to you now. I set off into the landscape
of Roslin Valley in Scotland with the intent of finding an animal ally that would work
with me in the otherworld. I wanted to see that magick could manifest in the physical
world, to prove to myself that it wasn't merely a creation of my imagination or a psychological illusion. I had no mobile phone, nor did anyone know where I was, and the
landscape was unfamiliar so there was an added element of risk. After walking a short
distance into the wooded valley, I heard the hooting of an owl—rather surprisingly, as it
was the middle of the day. The owl followed me for some time, moving from tree to tree
in the branches above my head. As amazing as this was (and the ally has stayed with me
to this day), I knew that there was more to come.

It was an incredibly wet day, with the kind of heavy summer rain that thoroughly
drenches you to the point at which you no longer care, as you know you can't get any
wetter. As I wound my way down the valley, a movement caught my eye down by the
stream many metres below—an otter? I leaned over on the muddy bank to get a better look and slipped. I started to slide uncontrollably down the steep, wet slope, catch-
ing hold of thorns and brambles to slow my fall. After sliding down about thirty feet, I
finally managed to stop. There was still about the same distance again to travel downwards before I reached the valley floor, and no way to scramble back up to the path in

the wet conditions. After mulling it over for some time, I realized that I would have to keep sliding, giving up control and trusting the journey. Eventually, much relieved and unharmed save for a few scratches and bruises, I reached the valley floor, full of joy and amazement at my adventure.

Then the most wonderful thing happened. The sun came out and shone in a dazzling golden ray onto the stream. It was shining directly onto a beautiful red deer that was standing in the stream and looking right at me; I knew I had found what I was looking for. The experience left me in no doubt, and I treasure the memory to this day.

EXERCISE: *Walking in Awareness*

Choose a location to begin your journey. This does not necessarily need to be somewhere familiar to you; indeed, I recommend when you are confident in the technique to try it in places that are completely new to you, but it is advisable to start somewhere where you will be undisturbed. If, as the journey goes on, you do encounter people, treat them as part of your journey. Wisdom and insights can come from unexpected places! Begin with the Faery Tree exercise as featured earlier in the book, drawing energy from above and below to meet in your centre. See the energies meeting at your heart centre in a warm golden light. Now, instead of releasing the energy back to the above and below, allow the golden light to grow and expand around you. Keeping your breathing steady, see the light reach from you, into your surroundings, in tendrils. These tendrils reach in all directions, connecting to the life around you. The light mingles with the energies of trees, of bushes, and of any creatures or energy beings in the area.

Can you feel a response from the life that you connect with? You can choose to either stay with this moment and then allow the energy to return to you, releasing it to the above and below, or you can hold on to this awareness and start to move forward into the landscape. If you are standing at a gateway, be aware of the gateway as an entrance into a new space, a new level of awareness.

Using the tendrils as a guide, feel your way through the landscape. Where does the energy draw you? Are you pulled along a path? Are you drawn to connect with a particular place on the landscape? Pay close attention to all around you…every breeze, every quivering leaf, every sound of a passing bee or bird. This is all part of the greater pattern of existence, the web of life in which you are now an active and aware part. Look at every detail. Listen intently to every sound. Where are you being led? What are you being told? Savour every fragrance in the air and every texture. Touch and feel the bark, the grass, the moss. Rub leaves between your fingers.

We are surrounded by a world of amazing sensory experience that we are often closed to, our minds busy with our lives and other matters. All this mental clutter is put aside, all that is now is the moment, the place where you are now and the feelings you are experiencing. Allow yourself to be guided by sensation and energy through the landscape. Look with both your inner and outer senses. Uncover your own adventure. Make connections and discoveries or simply find the peace of oneness. Pay attention...trust... if you truly pay attention, you will not get lost (unless you are meant to).

When you are ready, return to your original location, bring your tendrils back into your centre, and return the energy back to the above and below, thanking the land and its spirits for the experience. Sit with the experience for a while, and make any notes that you wish. A drink and a small bite to eat, or rubbing your hands in salt, should ground you. Though everyday life cannot be conducted in this intense level of awareness, your everyday awareness and sensitivity will naturally be expanded. This exercise can and should be repeated on a reasonably regular basis and in different locations.

Suggested Activities

Practice
Perform the exercise Walking in Awareness as featured above at least once during this month. If possible, try doing it during different phases of the moon, and make notes on any differences in energy and experiences.

Experiment
Experiment with a number of different dowsing techniques, and compare results. Find a simple technique that works best for you.

Create
Using the techniques covered in this chapter, find a natural object that you feel will help you connect to your Faery ally. For example, if your ally seems particularly earthy, you may choose a stone, pebble, or piece of wood, or if they seem connected to the element of air, perhaps a feather, and so on. Obviously, if there is a definite combining of

elements, you may choose to combine a couple different items. Be sure to reach out to the spirits of place with your heart and mind and ask permission before you take anything, and leave something in its place if it feels necessary.

Now you may choose to embellish your object as much or as little as you like, to empower it with a personal creative touch. Perhaps if a symbol comes to mind that relates to your ally, you could paint it onto your item, or you could decorate it in any way that seems appropriate to you, bearing in mind keeping it as natural and organic as possible.

CHAPTER FOUR
Honour

"The nature of those spirits, or Elves, is they are affected with
and Love all those that Love them, & hate all those that hate
them; yea they Know both our minds & thoughts in a great
measure, whereby it comes to pass, that we may Easily Move
them to come to us, if we Rightly understand the Rules thereof."

The seventeenth-century Sloane MS 3825

• • • • • • •

In this chapter we will look at ways we can best honour our relationship with Faery and the world around us. This most important quality, so often neglected in our modern consumerist society, is connected to the sun and the direction of within. The symbolism of this assignation in itself says much about the focus of these pages. The sun represents the centre of our spiritual being and our own innate divinity. Just as the actual sun brings light, warmth, and life to the world, dispelling shadows of illusion, so we should draw on and express that energy within ourselves, casting off lies, doubts, betrayal, and deception to shine with an inner light of truth and honour. If we live our lives true to this inner radiance, then the Faery beings, spirits of place, and ancient gods will sense it and respond accordingly.

Here we will cover in detail the all-important subjects of shrine building and offerings, as well as a reminder of the importance of etiquette when dealing with Faery.

Shrines

To create a permanent sacred space that honours your Faery allies and strengthens your connection with them, you may wish to build a shrine, either within a special designated area of your home or (more appropriately for work with Faery) in an outdoor space. This can be as subtle and minimalist or as extravagant and over the top as you like—it is your personal expression of your devotion to Faery.

A shrine becomes a focal point for your interactions with Faery. Through regular use and leaving of offerings, it will become a meeting point between the worlds, and Faery beings and elemental spirits will be attracted to it. For this reason, if you choose or are compelled by circumstance to build your shrine within your home, do try to keep it as far as physically possible from any electrical items, especially computers! Not only will they play havoc with your equipment, but the electrical energy interferes with their ability to interact with you clearly as well. Imagine it as being rather like static noise or crossed lines on a telephone.

A common problem that some people have is that they share their space with people who may not be very understanding of their beliefs. Your shrine can be a simple as a painting or a single statue on a table or shelf. If it serves as a point of focus and you can regularly burn a candle or some incense near it, it can be just as potent a shrine as the most flamboyantly decorated creation.

Most shrines tend to build up over time around a main focal point, for which I recommend a statue, painting, or photograph. If there is a painting or photograph that transports you or that gives you feelings or impressions when you spend time looking at it, that will be perfect. Be creative and let yourself be inspired; shrine building can be fun!

Candles (remember never to leave them burning unattended), statues, crystals, stones, and objects collected from nature can combine to make a beautiful sacred space. You may also choose to keep your Faery Craft tools on your shrine (more about these in the next chapter), as once they have been dedicated you would be well advised to keep them in a special place and not let others touch them (unless you feel called to do so or it is under special circumstances). Certainly if you have space it is a good idea to have representations of the four elements on your shrine. Although you will probably accumulate all kinds of bits and bobs over time and your shrine may become quite abundant (cluttered), try to keep it as clean and tidy as you can to keep the energy pure.

EXERCISE: *Building a Faery Shrine*

As you have already read, there are no dictatorial rules for your shrine. Indeed, the more personal it is to you, the better. However, here are some ideas to get you started...

The first consideration must be location. Will yours be an outdoor or an indoor shrine, or will you have both? Outdoor shrines are preferable as good focal points for offerings, and indoor shrines are useful places to keep sacred objects that wouldn't last outdoors, as well as a focus for meditation. You should choose somewhere that will be undisturbed, easy to keep clean, and as peaceful as possible.

Gather the items that you wish to form the foundation of your shrine, bearing in mind that natural materials are preferable. If you have been working your way through all the exercises and activities in the book so far, you should have a number of objects with which to build your shrine. It is a good idea to have a single focal point, such as a painting or statue, and then build around that, adding objects in such a way that are aesthetic and meaningful. Before you begin, be sure that the area is clean and free from clutter. You will also need a chalice or bowl of water (from a natural source such as a spring, lake, river, or the sea, if possible) and some incense. You may use these initially to cleanse the energy of the space (see next chapter for more details if you are uncertain), and you will also need them at the end.

The placing of each object should be done with focus, positive intent, and significance. To use the objects from your previous activities and exercises as an example (this works best for an indoor shrine; use your judgement as to what items will withstand being left outdoors), you may wish to use your creative piece based around the symbol of your choice as a central focus. To the north of this, you may wish to place your clay object that you made to represent your experiences of the element of earth, with your painting of water to the west, your poem or song for air written neatly and placed in the east, and a candle in the south. Choose which direction best suits your Faery ally, and place the object that you found and decorated for them in an appropriate place. This gives you a good starting point, and shrines do tend to grow and change over time—for example, an indoor shrine may be an excellent place to keep your Faery tools, which will be covered in the next chapter, Magick.

Once you are happy with the way that your shrine looks, light your candle and call your Faery ally to you to help with the dedication. With incense burning, take your

water and, using your fingers, sprinkle it lightly three times over your shrine. Words or a song of dedication or even a dance may come to you as you do this. Ask your ally for inspiration. It may be as simple or as elaborate as you wish, but it should be heartfelt, dedicating your shrine to your Faery Craft. If at this stage you feel drawn to make any promises connected to your ally and your work with Faery, be sure that you will be able to keep them. If your shrine is outdoors, this is a good time to make a hearty offering of wine or mead!

Once you have completed this work, sit quietly in contemplation with your shrine for some time before blowing out your candle and thanking your allies.

Offerings

One of the most practical and effective ways of strengthening or building your connection with the Faery realm is through offerings. This is an area that seems to prompt far more questions than it does helpful answers, so I will address this issue in detail here. Let's start with the fundamentals.

An offering is a gift of energy from you to the beings you wish to build a relationship with. It is therefore important to consider what you can give that they will appreciate and respect. It is also extremely important to consider the impact of your offering upon the physical environment, as the spirits of that place will not work with you if you do not show respect for the area over which they are guardians. For example, if you are leaving a plate of food for them, remember to be certain that any creature that comes along will not be harmed by eating any of that food. Faery beings will sometimes take the form of physical creatures, "borrowing" their bodies or sending them as representatives, and of course it is of utmost importance to live with awareness and respect for all living things when working with Faery. Continuing with this example, once the food has been out for one night, then the offering is complete. If it has been accepted it will either have been consumed by creatures or the energy inherent in the food will have been taken out by the Faery beings. Any food that remains the next day must be either buried, burnt, or disposed of appropriately and not left to rot on the shrine or site. Any remains or debris left on a shrine or sacred site detracts from the purity of the energy, gives disrespectful signals to the spirits of the place, and can only attract negativity.

For offerings to be most effective, it is helpful to really put some thought into them. Think about what it is that you contribute creatively to the world, what your strengths are, and how you can incorporate that into your offerings. For example, if you enjoy baking, then you could make cakes or bread with appropriate herbs (remembering, of course, to burn or bury them after one day/night). A writer may wish to write and recite a poem, an artist may paint or draw something in their honour, a singer may sing a song. Indeed, we all have a unique energy signature that is carried in our voice, and one of the very best ways to connect with Faery is through singing from the heart, even if you don't consider yourself a singer. It is not for the judging outside world to hear, it is for the Faery beings, and they hear with their hearts. Through song we can directly connect our energy to theirs, and you may find that the more you use your voice in this way, the stronger both your voice and Faery connection will become. The great advantage of song as an offering is, of course, that it is always with you and leaves no trace in the environment.

Offerings are very closely tied in to the concepts of sacred space and spirits of place. To build a strong relationship with your allies and the spirits where you live and wish to do your magickal work, you should leave regular offerings in the same place, at the same time, and in the same way. If you have a garden, then it would be a good idea to have a special part of that garden put aside for your offerings. Ideally you can build a simple shrine, but of course that is not possible for everyone, nor is it essential. Faery is a path that does not require trimmings or tools but integrity, truth, and purity of intent.

If you do not have a garden, then find a particular area, tree, or plant within the land around you where you feel the energy of nature most strongly, then spend as much time there as you are able and use that space for your offerings and as a meeting point in this world between you and the Faery realm. Be aware that if you do set yourself a regular routine, it is important to maintain it or you may inadvertently cause offense. To begin with it is best to start with a regular monthly offering that is easy to remember, perhaps at the full moon. As you develop, you will find that your relationship with different beings at different sites will grow, and your way of leaving offerings will adapt according to the responses you receive.

Some Suggestions and Important Dos and Don'ts

A Bowl of Cream or Milk

This is a traditional household offering, particularly at the full moon, as the offering mirrors the appearance of the moon. Always use fresh full-cream milk, and give them the first of any bottle/carton if you can. This is an easy routine to maintain, and any remaining milk can be poured directly onto the land the next day.

Alcohol

Always a welcome offering! You may choose to give a whole bottle (or more) on a special occasion—for example, if you wish to ask permission for the spirits of place on a sacred site to perform a ritual. As a regular household offering, though, it is a good idea to give a portion of the alcohol that you are consuming as an act of sharing with your Faery cousins. Again, try to give them the first of the bottle if you can, and avoid drinks with too much artificial or chemical content. For example, a good wine, ale, or mead would make an excellent offering, but not an alcopop!

Cakes and Bread

Again, always welcome. Ideally these should be made by yourself so that they are imbued with your energy. Like the alcohol, you may wish to develop a household tradition of giving the first share to the faeries. Shop-bought is okay if it's not full of yucky preservatives, so if you must use shop-bought, do try to make sure that it is simple and wholesome fare. Consider that if you do not bake yourself whether there might be something else you could give or do that would be more personal.

Incense

The burning of carefully chosen herbs, barks, and resins on charcoal is an excellent offering provided you do not leave it to burn unsupervised (in case of fire) and that you remember to clear the ashes afterwards. Of course it is preferable that the incense is blended with an appropriate magickal focus, and it's particularly potent if sourced and blended yourself. If you are a keen gardener, you can grow and dry your own herbs for this purpose, thus connecting you and your offerings intimately with the land. Stick incense can be used, but try to make sure that it is all-natural and not full of artificial chemicals.

Music and Song

If you play a portable instrument, this is a wonderful way to express your dedication to the Faery path and pay tribute to your allies and the spirits of place. As already discussed, song is an excellent offering and way of connecting with their realm. Different beings have a particular fondness for certain instruments or types of music, and that is discussed in more detail elsewhere in the book. You may find that tunes and words come to you as you play and sing; this is the Faery beings sharing their gifts with you, and this becomes a two-way exchange and potentially a powerful connection. When you start to receive such inspirations, this is a good sign that a being wishes to form a relationship with you as an ally.

Dance

You might feel a bit silly going out into nature and dancing to no music! However, if you do find yourself moved by a sense of the rhythm of nature and the music that emanates from all living things and the otherworld itself, then dance can be the purest gift of all. Dance is an expression of energy that, like song, comes straight from the heart. You don't need to be a great dancer if you are open and pure of intent. Dance is also a very good way of keeping energized and grounded in your body when dealing with the Faery realm, which can at times be draining and disorienting if we lose our balance.

Candles

Burning a candle either in your house or out in nature is fine, but remember to not leave it unsupervised and to clean away your candle stubs afterwards. Natural beeswax is best.

Creative Acts

Even if you are not normally creative in any obvious way (everyone has the potential for some form of creative expression), you may wish to create something as an offering. A painting, model, or sculpture may become the focal point of your Faery shrine, or you may choose to create something from natural materials that will, in time, be taken into the landscape. It is best not to do this at sacred sites, however, which should be kept clean and pure for all, both of this world and the otherworld. A piece of writing may be recited and either kept for future work with Faery or burnt to send it to the otherworld.

Wildflowers

Opinion is divided on whether cut flowers are an appropriate offering in Faery work. I would urge you instead to plant wildflower seeds that encourage bees and butterflies and bring beautiful, growing life to the land rather than take the life of a growing thing. Certainly shop-bought flowers are an absolute no-no both for offerings and as altar dressing, unless they have come from a reliably organic local source. Most flowers on sale in stores have been imported from countries with poor working conditions and intensive chemical treatments. If you wish to use flowers on your altar, if possible they should be grown in your own space, not taken from the wild or bought from a shop. Fragrant herbs grown specially for the purpose in your own space are a good alternative.

Shiny Things

Coins or jewellery may be left, but it is important to really use your judgement as to whether it is appropriate in individual circumstances. Again, sacred sites should be left pure unless there is a longstanding tradition of offerings being left. If you feel called to leave something of great personal value, that is far more fitting than buying something specifically to give away, as it is more the energy and the act than the object itself that is a gift. Also be aware that through your giving, the spirits of place may intend for the object to pass on to another who will find it. This is all part of walking in awareness of the greater patterns of the web that unfold around us.

Acts of Devotion to Nature

Acts of physical labour out in nature may be dedicated to your work with Faery allies or they may ask you to undertake certain tasks. This can be as simple as leaving food out for the birds, picking up litter in your local area, or planting trees. Certainly when you have found your particular sacred space or spaces where you best connect with Faery, you should undertake to keep them in an orderly fashion and free from human debris. Keep an old carrier bag with you to take rubbish home in! A similar idea would be to donate money to an environmental cause.

Bodily Fluids

We may be a bit squeamish about bodily fluids and so on, but an offering of saliva, a tear, a drop of blood, menstrual blood, or even hair can be an excellent offering if accompanied by the right intent, usually to seal a pact or promise rather than as a gift. Giving from your body in this way is an act of trust, as to an extent it is giving the spirits of the place access to your energy signature that can be used against you if they have cause (for example, if you break a pact or a promise). Because an offering of this nature forms a powerful physical link with the land and spirits of place, do think carefully before it is used as to whether you can maintain that link and commitment (especially with blood; no more than a drop or two is needed or advised).

Things to Avoid

Glitter

Glitter is fine in its proper place—on your face! As most glitter is made of tiny bits of aluminium, plastic, and glass, leaving it out in nature is not only littering but very damaging for any wildlife that may ingest it. Edible glitter is a biodegradable alternative that should always be used when making children's bottles of "fairy dust," as they will inevitably want to pour it on flowers and plants.

Chocolate

Many well-meaning people leave chocolate as an offering out in nature, and even some so-called authorities on the subject recommend it. YOU MUST NOT UNDER ANY CIRCUMSTANCES LEAVE CHOCOLATE OUT IN YOUR GARDEN OR ANYWHERE IN NATURE! Because of the high amount of theobromine it contains, chocolate is extremely toxic to most animals, sometimes even deadly. I'm sure you can understand why it would be a highly inappropriate offering. Make sure you leave it out of any baked goods you leave as offerings too.

Leftovers

When leaving food or drink out for the faeries, it must always have been specially made for them or be the first and best portion (if necessary, it can be put to one side to be left out for them later). Giving them what is left over after you have eaten or drunk first is not an offering, it's a sign of disrespect. The same applies to any offering given because it's something that you no longer have a want or a need for.

The Neglected Shrine

If you are going to have a shrine—either in your dwelling place or preferably in your garden—it should always be kept clear. Food offerings should always be cleared the next day, as described earlier, and it should be kept free of any debris or mess. Neglected shrines attract negative energy and mischief (the bad kind)!

Crystals

Crystals are actually fine in your own space, either in your home or your garden shrine. It is recommended to check with your supplier to make sure they have been mined ethically. There is an unfortunate trend in modern times to leave crystals or even bury crystals at sacred sites. This is, of course, well-meaning, but it interferes with the natural energy network of such sites and as such is not advised as an appropriate offering. Sometimes a simple pebble charged with your own energy might be accepted by the spirits of place.

Timing

It is advisable to maintain a regular routine of offerings, even if it is just monthly or a few times a year, as well as when you feel the call to do so. The most important times to leave offerings for Faery is at the ancient Celtic festivals of Beltane (May 1, Northern Hemisphere; October 31, Southern Hemisphere), Midsummer (June 21, Northern Hemisphere; December 22, Southern Hemisphere), and Samhain (October 31, Northern Hemisphere; May 1, Southern Hemisphere). It is at these times that the veil between worlds is tangibly at its thinnest. If you work within another tradition that has dates particularly associated with faeries or spirits, then you should be sure to give offerings at those times. The phases of the moon have a magick that is above any details of human culture, so you may wish to leave offerings for the Faery beings at full moons and new moons particularly.

Remember...

Honour is not only in your outward acts towards Faery but is carried within you at all times.

Respect the everyday as much as the obviously magickal, for there is potential magick in every act and thought; all deeds both within and without send out ripples of consequence. A wise man once said to me, "You must wear your marigolds (rubber gloves worn for housework) at the same time as your crown," meaning you must always keep grounded, not take yourself too seriously, and see the wonder in the mundane! I've never forgotten that, and it has served me well.

Always keep your promises, and don't ever make promises you can't keep. This goes for the everyday as well as with Faery! For one thing, they'll know. For another, once you are on a path, you cannot choose to step on and off it to suit yourself. Learn to select your words carefully, and act within awareness.

Do not lie. Faeries may have a reputation for being mischievous and even amoral, but they do not lie. If they have been called deceptive it is because of their skills of glamour and illusion, but through the use of these they teach us much about ourselves if we are willing to listen, and we can start to see through the layers of illusion to the core's light of truth.

When we can walk the path with truth and honour, we gain insight and knowledge not only of Faery but of our true selves. That is when we are ready to embrace magick.

Suggested Activities

Create

Perform the main exercise for this section, Building a Faery Shrine, and be sure to maintain it, keeping it clean and tidy. Lighting a candle, burning some incense, or placing the occasional new object on your shrine are ways of strengthening your bond with Faery and your allies. Your shrine will now be your point of focus for any daily practice you have developed.

Practice

Have a good think about what you can best give, and try to get into a regular rhythm of leaving offerings. Experiment with offerings during different cycles of the moon and make notes of any fluctuations of energy or response.

Respect

By now you should have identified at least one potential outdoor sacred space that is important to you. When you visit this space, try to remember to take a bag with you to clear any rubbish there might be in the area, and always act respectfully. Consider ways in which you might actively care for your local environment, including local groups and volunteering.

CHAPTER FIVE
Magick

"I remember…I walked in Merlin's footsteps, sometimes
halting, sometimes fleet, with bright tremendous
Powers and old Enchantment spiced with fear…"

Rosaleen Norton, *Thorn in the Flesh*

• • • • • • •

We now look to the direction of below, the moon, and the quality of magick (the "k" is used here simply to distinguish between true magick and stage magic). The cycles of the moon affect us all and are of great importance in magick, ruling the realm of dreams and instincts. But what exactly is magick? Indeed, even seasoned practitioners still debate the definition—and since there are so many paths, techniques, and practices, it is no wonder! On its most essential level, magick is the art of causing transformation according to will. This transformation must always begin with the self, for when the self is in balance and connected with the inner and outer worlds, then energy is free to flow in accordance with the will of the individual. Hence, if you have been performing the exercises featured in previous chapters, you have already set foot on a magickal path, as you have begun the process of self-transformation with the aid of the elements, the spirits of the land, and your Faery allies.

Each chapter builds on the next, so in this chapter we will cover the subjects of sacred space, tools, and consecration, and bring all our acquired knowledge and experience so far to bear in some simple magickal exercises.

The magick of Faery Craft is not attached to or dictated by any particular doctrine or religion, nor is it in discordance with any particular path (other than fundamentalists of any religion that may have their issues with aspects of it), so it is purely a matter for your personal judgement whether it is for you. Certainly you do not need to be Pagan or Wiccan in order to practice these skills. This is wisdom of the land and its intrinsic energies, and thus it is open to all who feel the call.

The Seven Directions and Sacred Space

In order to be connected to the inner spiritual dimensions of the landscape, it is helpful to be aware of the interplay of the elements around you and your place in the universe. We are taught to be humble and not self-centred, and indeed we are all just a small part of the vast, unknowable span of existence. However, we are a part of that universe, and no part can be insignificant. Without the sum of its many parts, existence would not be. We are all of us the weavers of our own web of existence, all the centre of our own magickal universe. This is a key understanding when seeking for connection and awareness.

When we consider this, we can visualize ourselves as a central crossroads where the directions and their elemental correspondences meet. A number of magickal traditions work with the four directions and their elements as east (air), south (fire), west (water), and north (earth). In Faery Craft we expand this to include the additional dimensions of above, below, and within.

East

East is associated with the element of air, and hence with sylphs. It is the direction of new beginnings, clarity, truth and inspiration. The east rules over the mental faculties. When you call on the east, visualize the colour yellow or gold and imagine a cool breeze coming from that direction. Feel the power of the breath entering and leaving your lungs.

South

South is associated with the element of fire, of which the elemental being is salamanders. This direction brings the qualities of will, passion, and action. The south rules our creative and passionate drives. When you call on the south, visualize the colour red and feel glowing warmth coming from that direction. Feel the power of the electrical impulses within your body and the energetic potential contained within your centre.

West

West is associated with the element of water and the elemental beings called undines. The qualities brought by water include wisdom, understanding, intuition, and healing. Water rules over the emotions and instincts. When you call on the west, visualize the colour blue and the sound of running water or waves coming from that direction. Feel the flow of the water within your own body and how your emotions are affected by your surroundings.

North

North is associated with the element of earth and the qualities of endurance, stability, patience, and nurture. The elementals connected with this direction are gnomes. Earth rules over the physical body, your flesh and bones. When calling on the north, visualize the colour green, see and feel the presence of a mighty forest, and feel the stability of the earth beneath your feet.

Above

Above is the celestial realm, source of divine wisdom and the angelic and planetary powers. Above is the realm of our spiritual destiny and aspiration. When calling on the above, see a clear night sky and hear the song of the stars.

Below

Below is the realm of the ancestors, those who have walked these paths before us. It is also the land of the shining guardians of the inner, primal earth, the sidhe. When calling on the below, remember that every step we take is on the shoulders of the ancestors, and the land is made from their bones and blood. See a primal, vibrant landscape untouched by time and progress, and hear the deep, slow heartbeat of the land.

Within

Within is at the same time the divine celestial spark within ourselves and the spindle at the centre of all existence. When calling on the within, contemplate the vastness of the void and the huge potential of the divine self. Picture yourself as a star amongst a web of stars, and see the connecting energy between them all, with yourself at the very centre.

TOP: **south/fire**

LEFT: **east/sky**

TOP: north/earth
RIGHT: west/water

Creating Sacred Space

There are many reasons why one may wish to create a temporary sacred space and various different methods by which to do so, a few of which are detailed below to give you an idea of different techniques. You may wish to do this if you are consecrating tools, performing divination (e.g., reading the runes, ogham, or tarot), creating offerings, working any kind of magick, or simply desiring a space in which to focus and connect. If conducting any kind of formal magickal work outside in nature (for example, group ritual or spell work; your solo meditations and connection exercises will be fine), you must ask permission from the spirits of place first and bring offerings. I strongly recommend building connections with a particular location for this purpose (see Finding Your Power Place, page 105).

Remember to use the power of your voice. This does not necessarily mean excessive volume, but it does mean speaking from your centre with conviction. If you are timid and afraid to be heard, you will not be!

Purifying the Space

If performing any kind of magickal or meditation work within your home, be sure that the space is not only physically clean and tidy but also energetically clean. A simple method of doing so is to use incense (frankincense will do) or a smudge mix such as lavender, sweetgrass, and sage. If you are able to grow these herbs yourself at home, then that is even better! Take a portable censer, ceramic dish, or large shell and fill it with a layer of earth to absorb the heat. Then, placing a lit charcoal disc on top of your earth, add your herbs or incense. Using a feather or fan, make sure the smoke reaches every part of the room. It is a good idea to regularly perform this simple rite throughout your home to keep the energies pure. Don't worry, you won't misplace anything that is welcome and meant to be there. You can also then seal this purification by going around the room a second time but with blessed salt and water or water from a holy well or spring if you have it, simply flicking drops of water with your fingers and tracing your preferred symbols of protection around the walls, doors, and windows. If you do not have a preferred symbol, I recommend the pentagram.

EXERCISE: *Calling in the Seven Directions*

This is the equivalent of asking for their blessing and creating a simple circle; it's not a full invocation.

Facing the east, raise your hands, palms facing forwards, and say:

I call to the east and the element of air! Grant us your qualities of clarity, logic, and inspiration here today/tonight…hail and welcome!

Turn clockwise to face the south. Raise hands, palms forward, and say:

I call to the south and the element of fire! Grant us your qualities of action, transformation, and will here today/tonight…hail and welcome!

Turn clockwise to the west. Raise hands, palms forward, and say:

I call to the west and the element of water! Grant us your qualities of emotion, intuition, and wisdom here today/tonight…hail and welcome!

Turn clockwise to the north. Raise hands, palms forward, and say:

I call to the north and the element of earth! Grant us your qualities of stability, nurture, and stamina here today/tonight…hail and welcome!

Reach and face the above. Say:

I call to the above, the stellar realm! Realm of the stars, the angels and the Divine, grant us your guidance and insight here today/tonight…hail and welcome!

Reach and face the below. Say:

I call to the below, the realm of the ancestors and the luminous beings of the inner earth! Grant us your wisdom, power, and knowledge here today/tonight…hail and welcome!

Bring your hands and focus to the heart of self, saying:

**I call to the within, to the divine spark, to the star
within, to the spindle within the void by which we are all
connected! Grant the insight of the true self and the power
of connection here today/tonight…hail and welcome!**

When closing, perform in reverse order, turning anticlockwise, and revise the statements to "we/I give thanks for" instead of "grant us" and end with "hail and farewell!"

EXERCISE: *Casting a Circle*

You can use this technique in addition to the above or as a stand-alone technique for creating sacred space.

The raw basis of the technique is as follows: using your wand, dagger, or finger as an extension of your will, stand in the east of your circle. With your wand/dagger/finger extended at full arm's length in front of you, visualize an electric blue light coming from the point as you walk a complete clockwise circle and then eventually joining up at the point where you began. When your work is done, repeat the process in reverse, tracing the circle in an anticlockwise direction, taking the energy back into yourself.

The key to the effectiveness of this technique is energy, intent, and focus. You may find that words or song come to you as you focus—that there is a chant or rhyme that works for you—or that you prefer to cast your circle in silence.

It may suit you to declare your intention in a straightforward way, like so:

**I cast this circle as a boundary of protection and
power, creating a space between the worlds.**

Or you may prefer something more elaborate, such as this rhyme calling on the elementals to protect your space (remember to thank and dismiss them upon closing the circle):

**To sylphs of air, I call to thee
Of harmful winds be circle free.
Salamanders who dwell in fire
Protect this space from ill desire.**

To undines of the sparkling wave
From all harm my circle save.
And gnomes of sturdy, ancient earth
Protect from those who know no worth.
The circle cast, the web is spun
Let nothing pass till work is done.

The Becoming the Faery Tree exercise featured earlier (see page 50), can also be used as a simple method to create sacred space when performed with that intent. However, for heavier work it is recommended to use something a bit more sturdy!

Tools

As mentioned, Faery Craft does not require expensive tools or garments, as it is a path of nature and the heart. However, you may find that certain objects wish to work with you as allies. Sometimes they will stay with you for a long time or perhaps only for a day. We must always remember that all things possess spirit and thus they do not belong to us, as we are all connected as part of a larger pattern. Therefore, it is up to the individual to be aware of when it is time to allow such tools to move on, either returning into nature from whence they came or passed to other respectful hands. As your awareness and sense of connection strengthens, you will be able to sense when an object wishes to work with you and when it wishes to move on. You will also become more keenly aware that often a simple pebble is far better than any shop-bought bauble and a twig far better than the shiny crystal-clad wand in that glass case!

Here are some potential tools that you may wish to incorporate into your practice:

Wands and Staffs

A traditional tool in many magickal paths, the wand acts as a focus for your energy and an extension of your will. They can be used for creating sacred space, drawing sigils in the air, and many other energy-directing functions.

A staff has a similar role but has the added quality of acting as a bridge between the sky and land, rooting you to your surroundings. If undertaking a walking meditation or journey out in nature, or when setting out with magickal purpose into the wilds, a staff can be a trusted and also very practical companion.

When working with Faery, it is most likely a wand or staff will choose *you*. Not in the Harry Potter sense of going into a shop and trying them until you find the one that makes your hair stand up like in an eighties pop video, but in the sense that it will be somewhere on your path, and you will simply know. Don't try or want too hard, but allow it to happen naturally, and one day you will most likely find yourself holding a piece of wood and simply knowing that it is for you. This is my personal preference, rather than cutting from living wood or buying from a shop, though I have been lucky enough to have been gifted beautifully crafted wands by dear friends over the years. You may choose to decorate or personalize your wand, perhaps with ribbons or paint. Consider whether you wish to add symbols of power, whittle or carve it to change its shape, or whether it is perfect just as you have found it.

Do not worry too much if you are unable to identify what tree your wand or staff comes from, but if you are able to discover it, then there may be some meaning and special qualities for you to be aware of. I would recommend a good tree identification guide and a couple good books on tree lore that relate to the kind of trees you may have growing in your part of the world. As a starting point, here is a very brief look at some trees traditionally associated with Faery that may be suitable:

Alder
The alder has very strong associations with Faery and must be treated with much respect. It is a very protective wood in a very warriorlike way and would be a good wand for a strong will.

Apple
Apple is sacred to the divine feminine, especially to many ancient wisdom goddesses. This tree of Avalon brings visions of the otherworld and connection with the healing powers of the inner earth.

Ash
Another warrior tree, ash is seen as possessing qualities of strength, endurance, and protection. Yggdrasil, the world tree of Norse culture, is an ash. This tree also has strong associations with masculine energy and the Horned God.

Beech

Beech is a powerful gateway tree for seekers in the quest for knowledge and wisdom. It is often associated in ancient British lore with the power of the serpent.

Birch

Birch is traditionally associated with beginnings and rebirth. It is a feminine energy and aids in travelling between the worlds. It is one of several trees associated with protection.

Blackthorn

Blackthorn is used for what is known as a "blasting rod"—a specialized wand with the power to bless or curse. Strongly connected with deep magick and the darker side of Faery, blackthorn is a powerful choice for a wand or staff and is not for the faint-hearted.

Elder

This tree is connected with powers of transformation and shapeshifting. It is seen as possessing or often being a feminine spirit capable of changing forms. However, a wand or staff made of elder may not last long.

Hawthorn

Deeply rooted in Faery lore, hawthorn is associated with spring and marriage rites. Its energy is not wholly dissimilar to its sister tree, blackthorn, only more connected with spirits and gods of fire and light than with darkness.

Hazel

A popular choice for wands and also water-dowsing rods, hazel is said to bring the gifts of eloquence and the power of divination. Deeply associated in folklore with ancient wisdom, it is one of several trees seen as being particularly potent gateways to Faery when growing in a pair.

Holly

Holly has a fiery and passionate energy that, when well managed, can be an excellent choice as a wand or staff to aid with energy building and as a focus for magickal work.

Oak

As one of the most revered and sacred trees in many cultures, oak is a sturdy choice for a wand or staff. Connected to the Green Man, Horned God, and the Dagda of Irish lore, oak is known for its magickal qualities of protection, particularly against fire or lightning.

Rowan

Rowan is said to protect against negative influence, so it would be a good choice if you do a lot of work clearing energy in troubled areas. It is connected to many solar and fire deities as well as having strong ties with Faery.

Willow

Willow is a traditional choice for wands, being a good balance of light and dark and having many magickal qualities. Connected to the moon and the element of water, willow enables communication with spirits and also has powers of healing.

Yew

With its associations with death, war, and poison, yew may not be everyone's first choice as a companion tool. However, if you are willing to walk the deeper path and connect to the inner drumbeat of the earth, yew has the power to bring the deep transformations needed.

Swords and Daggers

Those who are used to working in ceremonial magick groups may wish to use a sword or dagger in their work. However, it must be remembered that it offensive to most Faery beings to use iron in your work. Bronze, silver, or even wood can be a viable alternative. In most cases, the sword or dagger performs much the same functions as a wand. In ceremonial work they are used to command spirits (amongst other functions), but this is not a technique I recommend when trying to build a trusting connection with the realms of Faery! A sword or dagger may prove most distinctly useful when having to cut old connections or unwanted attachments that may form during the work. You also may wish to have a weapon of this kind made from traditional material (including iron) for use in the unlikely event of encountering unwanted attention from harmful Faery beings or other spirits. This should not be kept on your person or in any area of your living space where you hope to attract or work with Faery.

Enchantress Sorita D'Este wields her
ritual sword with the grace and power
befitting a Faery queen!
(photo courtesy of David Rankine)

Stones, Pebbles, and Crystals

Our friends from the mineral kingdom are more akin to allies than they are to simply being tools. They have an energy, a spirit, and (to an extent) a will and personality of their own, and this must be accepted before you can truly work with them. Expanding your awareness in order to be able to embrace and connect with a consciousness so different from your own is a valuable exercise that will certainly strengthen your work with and connection to the Faery realm. Pebbles may not appear to be as glamorous or enticing as crystals, but, again, a pebble found in a special place may hold more power than the shiniest crystal bought from a faceless shop.

Stones and pebbles have many uses, and as your awareness and connection to your surroundings strengthen, so will your intuitive awareness of the magickal potential and spirit of objects. A stone found in a place of power can be held in meditation or even just kept in your pocket to help you "plug in" to the energy of the place. (I hope I don't need to say that under no circumstances should you be chipping parts of standing stones or sacred structures of any kind for this purpose!)

Charging a pebble or crystal with healing energy and then putting it in water can create a healing elixir, or you may charge it with another intent—for example, clarified thinking or enhanced prowess. A stone may help to balance your energies or ground you after magickal work, or you could breathe your troubled thoughts into it and then wash them away. When you do find such allies to work with, spend time simply holding them and emptying your mind, letting them speak. They will most likely communicate to you what they would like to help you with.

If you choose to work with crystals, try to be sure that they have been ethically mined, for not only will the energy of ill-treated crystals be scarred and hard to work with, but it is also against the ethics of Faery work to use something that has been cruelly rent from the land. You don't need masses of all kinds and colours of crystal; a trusty piece of clear quartz will serve you well in most kinds of energy work. If you are looking for a crystal that is particularly associated with Faery, you may want to seek out a piece of staurolite. I also find that moldavite is a very powerful stone when wishing to channel the energies of the sidhe, but it may not be for everyone. If crystals are something you find particularly helpful, you may wish to try malachite and amethyst to aid in psychic awareness and meditation.

Hagstones, also known as holey stones, fairy stones, and wish stones, are stones that have a naturally worn hole running all the way through them. Most commonly found on beaches, they can also be found in streams or by rivers, as the hole is made by water eroding away the stone over many years. These are particularly potent items, most often hung around the home or worn on the person for protection. If you are lucky enough to find or be gifted a hagstone, thread some red wool the length of your arm through the hole and tie it into a loop, then hang it by your door; that will protect your home from any harmful energies.

Hagstones are also renowned as granting the ability to see Faery beings if you look through the hole. I would suggest that this is a simplified hint at a possible use in trance and journey work. Try holding the stone in your hand when out in nature, and then imagine yourself travelling through the hole as a gateway. See where it takes you…

Chalice or Bowl

Water, especially from springs and wells, is very important in magickal work, being used most often for clearing space, blessing (both space and individuals), healing work, protection, and to consecrate tools and other objects. Of course water needs to be contained, and a silver, glass, or wooden bowl or chalice should be dedicated purely for this purpose. If used for anything mundane in addition to your magickal work, the energies will become tainted and ineffective. Silver is most preferred due to its reflective qualities that aid in holding energy, particularly if charging your water with moonlight.

Drums and Musical Instruments

Faery beings enjoy music played by natural instruments rather than recordings. You will also find that different elemental beings will be attracted by different kinds of sound. For example, earth elementals find the sound of the drum appealing, whereas some water spirits enjoy voice and strings. (For more detail on this area, see the sections on the elements in chapter 2.)

Drums and music can also aid in creating altered states in which you may experience a heightened awareness of your surroundings and the spiritual beings within the landscape, so it is definitely worthwhile finding something that resonates with you. A simple, regular beat on a bodhran (a traditional Irish drum used in journey work) can be highly effective. The trick is to listen for the vibration between the drumbeats.

Glass Bottles

Many people use plastic bottles to gather water from springs, rivers, or the ocean for their work, as they are lightweight and convenient. Unfortunately, plastic is an unnatural substance made from polluting chemicals and is thus unsuitable as a container for magickal energy, so try to use glass bottles instead. It is fine to reuse bottles that originally contained other liquids, providing that they are thoroughly cleansed.

Offering Dish

As has already been covered in the previous section, offerings are an extremely important part of Faery Craft, so it is a good idea to have a dish or dishes (again, not plastic) that are used purely for this purpose.

Earth

When consecrating tools, it is most effective to bless them by the four elements. You may wish to use a special stone or rock for earth, but another idea is to have a small wooden or ceramic box in which you keep earth, leaves, small pebbles, and so on from places that hold special significance for you. You can even ask friends to send you small quantities of earth from different sites around the world. Do be careful who you ask, though, as the average person is liable to think this a slightly odd request! I have a small box of earth from the different Celtic lands, and I use this for consecrating and sometimes for offerings, as it was a gift at my ordination and is sacred to me.

Censer

Loose-grain handmade incense burnt on charcoal is far preferable to joss sticks, so you'll need either a censer or a ceramic dish dedicated to the purpose of burning incense. You may prefer something natural such as a large shell or even a flat rock on which you can place the burning charcoal disc.

Candles

A candle is the most obvious choice to represent the element of fire on your shrine or in any magickal work. If you can, try to get a special beeswax candle for use in consecrations.

EXERCISE: *The Consecration and Dedication of Tools*

Consecration need not be a hefty or complex process; indeed, it can be quite simple. There is no set technique for consecrating tools for working with Faery, and you may find and adapt your own methods based on this basic formula:

Set up your sacred space in your preferred method (see sections on sacred space and the seven directions earlier in this chapter). Be sure to have representations of the four elements on your altar. Incense is normally used to represent the powers of air, a candle (red if you wish to use a colour) for the powers of fire, a chalice or bowl of water for water, and either salt, earth, or a sacred stone for the powers of earth. If you have magickal oil you can also use this to represent the fifth element of spirit, which also acts as a seal of the other elemental blessings. If you don't have an altar, a special cloth that you bring out purely for this purpose and lay on the floor will be fine—just make sure that it is protected from any objects that may get hot, such as your censer if it is metal. Before you start, make sure that you have everything you need within your space.

You may wish to allow words or song to arise within you as you pass your tool or object through the elements, or you may wish to write something beforehand. You may use the following example as a foundation for developing your own personal practice:

By the east and the element of air I do bless this tool to bring clarity and truth to my Faery Craft. (*pass item through the smoke of the incense three times in a clockwise circle*)

By the south and the element of fire I do bless this tool to bring will and passion to my Faery Craft. (*pass item through the heat of the flame three times in a clockwise circle*)

By the west and the element of water I do bless this tool to bring healing and intuition to my Faery Craft. (*sprinkle item with drops of water three times*)

By the north and the element of earth I do bless this tool to bring stability and strength to my Faery Craft. (*either touch your item to the stone or sprinkle with earth or salt, depending on your preferred method*)

By the above, the realm of stars (*present to the above*), **and the below, the realm of the ancestors and sidhe** (*present to below*), **and by my own ineffable divine spark that dwells within and the stars within the land itself, by the spindle of the web, I dedicate this tool to my Faery Craft for as long as it will work with me.**

Thank the powers and close the sacred space.

Weaving Magick

Faery magick has three main strands. There is magick that is performed in the otherworld, there is magick performed in this world, and there is magick that weaves the two together, the latter being the most profound. Magick encompasses many forms and methods but mostly follows the simple formula of intent + focus + energy + action =

transformation. Thus the exercises throughout all the sections of this book are magickal, for they all use intent, focus, energy, and action in order to bring transformative powers into our lives, bringing us closer to connection and understanding.

All of the above elements are equally important and must be in balance for magick to be effective, just like the ingredients of a recipe or the elements of a car journey—if you have no fuel and you don't know the way, you won't be going anywhere even if you may know where you want to go. Equally, if you have fuel and a working vehicle and even a map but no idea where you want to go, you could end up anywhere. The outcome is unpredictable and the journey pointless, as much of a waste of energy as if you were to perform magick for the sake of it but without any real intent or focus. Even if you have a decent car, fuel, map, and an idea of where you want to get to, you have to drive it! Without action, all the intent, focus, and energy in the world will only remain within yourself.

Faery magick is essentially folk magick, simple and based in the world of nature. That, however, does not preclude exploration of other magickal paths in addition to Faery work; indeed, they can be complementary if the intent is in harmony and there is no conflict between practices. Knowledge expanded through a search for truth can only increase our understanding in other areas, all forming part of an enormous jigsaw puzzle. There are often as many moments of confusion and doubt as there are of illumination, if not more so, but with strength and persistence the light of truth is found and the patterns of connection become clear.

Faery Magick and the Elements

In Faery Craft we can use our understanding gained through contemplation of the elements and their different aspects as building blocks for practical magick. Here are some simple examples for you to try. You should recognise, within the simple formulae of these workings, the elements and the divisions of primal, living, and still that you were introduced to in chapter 2. A good connection with our Faery allies and the world around us can teach us many such possible applications, which are simple yet potent techniques. Once you have tried these examples, work with your Faery allies to expand upon these principles and create your own practices.

The following practical magick exercises show how, in Faery Craft, actions and instinctive connection with nature take the place of the human construct of "spells." As implied by the name, spells are constructs of words and symbols designed to combine with energy and intent to bring about a particular result. The practical magick of Faery Craft takes us into the realm of nature and is reliant on our connection with the elements and the hidden beings of the inner landscape. These workings are exceptionally simple in construct, the strength being in the action, energy, intent, and connection.

EXERCISE: *To Be Rid of Negative Thoughts*

Sometimes we can get caught in negative thought patterns that can affect our well-being and ability to focus. For this simplest of magickal workings, take a walk by living water—either a stream, a river, or a waterfall. Whilst walking, bring the troubling thought to the front of your mind. Form the thought with as much clarity and definition as you can. Does it have a shape? A colour? A scent?

When you have the thought defined within your mind and separate from the rest of your self (as well as you can manage this), find a small stick or piece of wood that has fallen near or on your path. Taking this piece of wood in your hand, stand by the running water and feel the connection with your surroundings.

Call upon your Faery ally by whatever method you feel works for you, either internally or through words or song. Asking your ally to aid you in ridding yourself of this troubling thought, focus on your intent and the thought in as much detail as you can, taking a deep breath.

With your piece of wood in both hands before you, visualise the negative thought and feelings associated with it leaving your body with your breath, and blow them into the piece of wood. Throw the piece of wood with as much force as you can muster into the water, then breathe in feelings of peace and unity from the landscape around you. Envisage the space that the evicted negativity has left behind being filled with golden light, making you whole once more.

Give thanks to your Faery ally, and walk on without turning back either physically or mentally. This exercise may be repeated over a number of days if necessary.

EXERCISE: To Aid in Healing

This may be performed on your own behalf or another's, but be sure that whomever you are intending to perform healing for has asked for your help, as healing should not be performed without permission. This practice will be most effective for ailments that are the result of infection or toxins in the system and can be combined with methods of hands-on healing as covered later in the chapter.

Find a palm-sized stone out in the landscape that you feel somehow represents the person in need of healing. Call on your Faery ally to aid you in this work. Focus on the person and their ailment with as much detail as you can, and breathe into the stone.

Next, either in a small pot or a location that you will easily find again, bury your stone in soil for one night, with the intent that any illness will seep out into the earth. The next day, take your stone and any soil that is still attached and wash it in living water—for example, a stream or a river—with the intent that you are washing away impurities. Hold your stone up to the sunlight and visualise the power of the sun filling the stone with golden light. You may now gift the stone to the person in need of healing so they may carry it with them or keep it close to their bed at night as a healing charm.

This working may be adapted with intent to heal a particular location rather than an individual, leaving the stone in that location when the work is complete.

The Importance of the Moon

The quality of magick corresponds with the moon and the direction of below on the Faery Craft septagram, and the moon and her cycles are indeed useful things to bear in mind in the practice of magick. When the moon is waxing or full, it is a good time for productive or creative magick, building towards a goal. When she is waning, that is a good time for any clearing of blockages or banishing magick. When the moon is completely new and in her dark phase, this is the best time for any kind of divination or channelling work.

The following simple magickal working builds on elements you should already be familiar with from earlier chapters. It is written here for the solo practitioner, but you may easily adapt it for group work if you wish. It is broken down into clear sections so that you can clearly see the structure. This will help you devise your own future ritual workings.

EXERCISE: *Full Moon Ritual*

Preparation

This ritual must be performed outside under the light of the full moon, so you will need a suitable location where you will not be disturbed. You will need a chalice of water (preferably silver if you can manage it, but certainly of a natural substance and not plastic). If you have a wand, you may wish to use this for the circlecasting. You will also need to have an offering of food and/or drink prepared, traditionally a saucer of full-cream milk, but look to the section on offerings for other ideas. You will need to be aware of the directions, using a compass if necessary. You will also need a glass or ceramic container in which to keep your water after the ritual.

The intent behind this ritual is to call on the energy of the moon, the seven directions, and your Faery allies to aid you in a creative goal for the month ahead, so be sure to have a positive goal in mind.

Greeting and Asking Permission

With all your tools and the offering prepared and accessible, centre yourself using the Becoming the Faery Tree exercise on page 50. Touch the fingers of your right hand (or left if you are left-handed) to your lips, heart, and forehead in turn as a greeting. With arms by your sides and palms facing forward, call to the spirits of the place:

> **Spirits of this place, people of peace, dwellers of the hollow**
> **hills, I humbly greet you and ask you to grant your blessing**
> **upon this work tonight. I bring you this offering as a gesture of**
> **cooperation. I honour you and the spirit within all things.**

Present the offering and give the triple salute again. Wait until you feel that your request has been accepted or declined. If declined, give thanks and farewell to the spirits of place and proceed no further. You may wish to try again in a different location. If accepted, proceed as follows:

Create Sacred Space

Use the circlecasting technique detailed on page 136. If working in a group, you may wish to call to the seven directions with different people calling to each direction.

Invocation

Raise arms in a V shape up to the moon, with your chalice of water ready.

> **Great Mother, mirror of the Source, gateway to the enchanted**
> **realm, I call to you! Blessed Queen of the tides of life,**
> **ruler of cycles both without and within, hear my call!**

Drawing Down the Moon into Water

Holding your chalice in both hands, raise it up high over your head so that the light of the moon is reflected in the surface of the water. Hold this position and will the power of the moon into the water as you speak:

**As your silver light descends into this cup, so may your blessing
fill this water. Imbue it with your great love so that it may
carry your magick and inspiration forth into the world.**

Hold for a short time. When you are confident that the power has entered the water, bring the cup back down. Use your forefinger to trace a septagram in visualised blue light above the surface of the water to seal it.

Blessing and Dedication

Described here for solo ritual, this may easily be adapted and performed by one member of a group as priest/ess, with another of the group performing the blessing on the priest/ess at the end. Simply change the wording in each case to "your" instead of "my." Hold the chalice of water in the left hand as you speak:

**I consecrate my body as a tool of creation
and inspiration for my Faery Craft.**

(face east)

**May the spirits of air bless my thoughts with
clarity and spiritual knowledge!**

(dip little finger of free hand into water and touch to forehead; face south)

**May the spirits of fire bless my centre so that my inner
flame of divine inspiration will always burn brightly!**

(dip little finger of free hand into water and touch to solar plexus; face west)

**May the spirits of water bless my heart so that it may be
open to the flow of truth and the purity of love.**

(dip little finger of free hand into water and touch to chest; face north)

**May the spirits of earth bless my hands so that they
may be tools of sacred creation within the world,
bringing the beauty of Faery into manifestation.**

(dip little finger of free hand into water and touch to centre of palms; face the above)

**May the spirits of the celestial realm bless my spirit so
that it may shine like a star as a beacon for others.**

*(dip little finger of free hand into water and touch to crown
of head; face the below, crouching down if possible)*

**May the spirits of the ancestral realm bless my feet so that they
may walk with respect upon the sacred earth and ever feel the
support of those who have walked these ways before me.**

*(dip little finger of free hand into water and touch to both feet;
rise, and hold chalice in both hands over your centre)*

**With the blessings of all the directions and my Faery allies, I will
carry this light into the world. May it shine through my every
action, through my work, and through every part of my being.**

(take sip of the water)

Close the sacred space and give thanks to the spirits of place. You may store the rest of
the water for use in other work.

Other Subjects to Explore

This is a huge area, and there is not enough room in this book to cover it all in detail.
In addition to the foundation techniques covered so far, I have highlighted some areas
that you may wish to explore in more detail if you feel called to do so. With the aid and
advice of your Faery allies, through journey and meditation, and also simply through
spending time in the landscape and being open to experiences, you may find yourself
being called to delve further into any of these practices.

Healing

If you use or feel drawn to try any kind of hands-on energy healing, this can be
greatly supported by connection to the land around you. I am particularly lucky to live

near a river and a holy well, and when healing I connect to their energy, feeling the power of the water flowing through me and clearing away energetic blockages.

Spirits of any of the elements may be able to help you in your healing work. Spirits of stone, hill, and mountain may help to bring stability and stamina or aid in healing bones, where the quality of stone is echoed in our bodies. Similarly, spirits of living earth may help with the healing of muscle and fleshy tissue. The energy of fire must be used with caution, but to have fire, or even just a candle nearby, to draw on when healing can add necessary focus and energy, bringing the light of hope to dark places. This connection can also be honed to purge unwanted energies but is not as gentle as water. Air, of course, can be called upon to help with respiratory ailments, and the power of breath can be used both to help in extracting what is not needed and bringing in favourable energies.

When performing healing, always be sure that you have the permission of the person in need of healing. Holding your hands a few inches from the patient's body, you may find that you can feel energetic tingles, blockages, cold and hot patches, or that images or even words come to you. Tune in to your Faery ally and trust your intuition. When you do place your hands on the patient, allow your breathing to become deep and steady, and focus on a nearby landscape feature or place of power, allowing the energy to flow through you.

Sigils

A sigil is a symbol created as a focal point for magickal intent. It can be a preexisting symbol or one specially created for the purpose. We have already seen with the great glyph of the sidhe how a sigil can act as an astral doorway into the otherworld. Sigils have a number of other uses, including as a point of focus for magickal work or for protection. You may wish to journey with your Faery allies to find suitable sigils for specific purposes, remembering to state this as your intent when journeying, or you can craft a sigil consciously for a purpose. To do this, consider the qualities that you wish to encapsulate, find or create suitable symbols for them, then merge these into the simplest possible form that you can, containing elements of all the symbols.

When using a sigil to protect the home, you may want to paint it on a stone or stones, empower it by breathing your intent and energy into it, then place it with intent near the entrance or windows of your home. To use a sigil as a temporary magickal focus, either draw it on a piece of paper or some other temporary form, such as sand on a beach. Imbue it by building up energy with focus, either through physical activity such as dance, breathing, or your preferred method, then destroying the sigil and thus releasing it into the universe. Drawing sigils on the beach is a lovely method, for you can focus on your sigil and then allow it to be washed away into the ocean by the waves on the shore.

Divination

We have already discussed the gift of prophecy and its strong connections to the realm of Faery, so naturally you may wish to train in a method of divination. There is no particular method that is most connected with Faery, so simply explore, listen to the guidance of your Faery allies, and find what works best for you.

If you connect particularly well to trees, you may wish to learn more of the ancient druidic alphabet called the ogham, which can be used for divination in a similar way to runes, which are another popular choice. If you are a strongly visual person, then I recommend acquiring a set of tarot or oracle cards that speak to you. There are a number of excellent sets available that feature Faery, and these can also act as a bridge to their realm for communication as well as for divinatory purposes.

Other possibilities include scrying into a pool of still water or into the embers of a fire. Simply still your mind and allow images, sounds, or words to form without judging them, and then interpret them later. Keep a journal of your efforts—this can be most helpful to look back on and compare results.

Dreams

Working with Faery tends to enhance dreams, and powerful messages may come that need to be acted on. Try keeping a regular dream diary to help you recognise recurring patterns and symbols. This not only trains your mind to recall dreams more easily, it can also lead to active lucid dreaming. This is a state of dreaming where we become aware that we are dreaming and thus are able to control our dream environment, which is a very useful tool for Faery work. You may also try sleeping with certain objects—say, an empowered pebble or crystal—beneath your pillow or near your bed to enhance your dream experiences.

Finding Your Gift

You may already have a good idea of where your strengths lie and what gifts you would bring to the world of Faery. Are you a healer? An oracle? A visionary? A bard, perhaps? All of us have particular areas that we are drawn to more than others, and these can be developed into a set of skills that benefit both our world and Faery. Consider what you have learnt so far, which exercises you felt worked best for you, and which qualities of the elements most resonated with you. These should give you some clues. There is no quick and easy path to self-knowledge, but the gift that takes time and effort to find is worth all the more, like a rare treasure in an archaeological dig. Keep strong connections with the land and your otherworldly allies, and this will help you uncover your potential. The following exercise was gifted to me by Faery to help you on your way…

EXERCISE: *The Apple Seed*

For this exercise you will need one apple, preferably locally sourced. Sit comfortably in a place where you will not be disturbed. Hold the apple in your hands, resting on your lap. Take three deep breaths and release all tension, then breathe steadily, relax, and close your eyes. See the apple in your mind's eye. Consider the apple as a symbol of knowledge, experience, and wisdom. Know that the skin of the apple is your outer self—all your day-to-day thoughts and mundane needs and responsibilities. See the skin peeling from the apple, leaving the flesh beneath. Discard the skin and, along with it, any of your mundane concerns of the moment.

Now you see the apple. Know that the flesh of the apple represents your acquired knowledge and experience of this lifetime, the world that you have built around yourself. You now see that the apple is divided into a top and a bottom half, and it splits into two halves along the horizontal, one half in each hand. Look at the revealed centre of both halves of the apple. In both halves you see the pattern of a five-pointed star, just as you would if you cut open an apple in physical reality. In one of the halves, you see five seeds in the star pattern.

The five seeds begin to glow. They may take on different colours and different levels of brightness. Something about one or more of the seeds draws you to it/them. Laying down the other half of the apple, take the seed or seeds out of the apple and place it in the palm of your hand. The seed changes shape and becomes a new object. This is a sym-

bol of your Faery gift, a part of your divine nature, what you are here to share with the world. Remember this symbol well. If it does not make sense now, study it, meditate on it further, and it will make sense in the future. Trust. The symbol becomes a seed once more. Ask your Faery ally or animal guide to take you to an appropriate location and plant the seed in the ground of the otherworld. When this is complete, return to your starting location and slowly return to normal awareness.

Open your eyes. Make any notes you need to and draw any symbols you have received. Now take the physical apple and cut it in half across the horizontal, revealing the five-pointed star and the seeds within. If you can, choose the corresponding seed to the seed or seeds you were drawn to in the meditation, or if that is difficult for whatever reason, choose whichever seed you are drawn to now. Take the seed and the two halves of the apple either to a personal power place or your outdoor shrine. Give one half of the apple as an offering, eat the other half yourself, and plant the seed in the ground as a sign of commitment to your Faery allies to develop and use your gift in both worlds.

Some Thoughts for Further Study

* Which direction or element did the position of your seeds correspond to on the pentagram? What is your relationship like with this element? What qualities do you associate with it?

* What does the symbol that you received mean to you? What other meanings might it have? List all the words and meanings you can think of connected to this symbol. Does it reveal anything unexpected?

* What location were you taken to in the otherworld? Did it resemble any real-world location you are familiar with? What significance might this have? Ask your guide in a future journey what the significance of this place is and what future work you have to do there, if any.

Suggested Activities

Practice

Perform the exercises as detailed in the chapter. Experiment by adapting them with your own wording, and make notes on your results.

Create

* Use Walking in Awareness to find a wand for use in your Faery Craft. Consecrate it as detailed in this chapter and decorate it as you see fit. You may choose to keep it on your Faery shrine.

* Once you are comfortable and confident in creating sacred space using the seven directions, write your own calls to the directions and circlecasting. Make notes on any changes of energy and effectiveness.

* Using the examples given in this chapter as a reference and your knowledge and experience of the elements so far, devise your own simple protection spell using a combination of three elements in their natural form.

Experiment

Call on your Faery allies to help you choose some different methods of divination. Record your results, and see which method works best for you and your ally.

Observe and Analyse

Start a diary, paying close attention to the changing cycle of the moon, and make notes of your own moods and energy levels. Keep a record of any significant dreams and also any magickal exercises, divinations, and spells attempted during each moon phase and their results. Entries need only be brief, but try to be disciplined, and remember to note any other factors such as health, exercise, diet, and so on. This should give you an idea of how the moon affects you through its different cycles.

CHAPTER SIX
Joy

In the sixth chapter we look to the west and the quality of joy, represented by the element of water. Water is the element of emotions, healing, and memory, and through the following pages we will look at different ways in which you may experience the most positive aspects of these qualities within the Faery community. So far in *Faery Craft* we have concentrated on skills and experiences that are practiced in isolation and with a serious and respectful attitude, yet there must always be room for fun and celebration! To share your love of Faery with others can be a deeply rewarding experience, and you will soon learn that beneath all the glitter and spangles of the Faery events there is real depth to be found.

We will look at taking your first steps into the Faery community and the first points of contact that are available, including magazines, the Internet, and the large variety of events that are ever-welcoming to new faces. We will speak with some key members of the Faery community and take an in-depth look at what you might experience at a Faery festival. We will then look at the deeper aspects of dressing up, which is so often dismissed as frivolous but can carry significance and bring both transformation and connection when performed with intent. While it's important to take our Faery Craft seriously, it is just as important not to take ourselves too seriously…so let your hair down. It's playtime!

"As I look, they seem to me like children of the wind and sunshine, leaping and running in these flowing pastures, with a laughter as sweet against the ears as the voices of children at play. The joy of life vibrates everywhere."

Fiona Macleod, *At the Turn of the Year, Essays and Nature Thoughts*

· · · · · · ·

Joy comes naturally as a part of practising Faery Craft, through connection with the landscape and our Faery allies, and from appreciation of the beauty and sanctity of our world. It also comes from connecting and celebrating with each other and realising that we are not alone in our beliefs and choice of lifestyle. The discovery of the vibrant Faery community, with its colourful characters and all-accepting nature, can be a revelatory experience for many, opening them up to a whole new world and bringing fresh confidence—and, yes, great joy!

Joining the Community

There are a number of magazines produced by and for the Faery community, including *Faerie Magazine* in the United States and *Faeries and Enchantment* (aka FAE) in the UK, both packed full of fascinating features and stunning artwork.

One of the more positive aspects of our modern technological world is the possibility of online social networking, with members of Faery communities all over the world building connections and friendships on sites such as Facebook and Twitter, which have taken the place of smaller online forums.

Image courtesy of Karen Kay

Even better than reading about the ins and outs of Faery frolics, why not join in? There are dozens of Faery events held throughout the year all over the globe, including festivals, balls, markets, and workshops. Try searching on the Internet to see if there are any events near you or within travelling distance.

Here's a brief look at some of the most prominent and notable regular events from around the world:

Canada
Enchanted Ground
Enchanted Ground is Canada's foremost annual outdoor faery festival which takes place in Guelph, Ontario. With all kinds of themed entertainment for families, this weekend event has something for everyone. For more information, visit www.faeryfest. com.

USA
Faerieworlds Events
Faerieworlds dominates the Faery scene in the United States, with numerous events over many states throughout the year, including Faeriecon, Mythic Faire, and an annual Harvest Festival, as well as the main Faerieworlds outdoor festival.

These are well-organised events with fascinating guests, exceptional entertainment, many talented artists and intriguing traders, with large numbers attending every year. For more information, visit www.faerieworlds.com.

NY Faerie Fest
New York Faerie Fest is a wholesome family event held in rural New York state. The focus is on nature, spirituality, and the arts, and there are performances from a variety of talented entertainers. A perfect choice if you have children, this outdoor event has a no-alcohol policy and lots to see and do for the whole family. For more information, visit www.nyfaeriefest.com.

photos on this and following page
©2011 Byron Dazey Creative Flashes
(used by the kind permission of Faerieworlds LLC)

> "I go every year to the Fairy and Human Relations Congress
> that's held in a very remote place in the mountains in eastern
> Washington, in a place called Twisp; 2012 will be its twelfth
> year! People dress up, and there's people of all ages, from
> grandparents down to teeny little children, and you see them
> in all sorts of costumes, but it's also very environmentally
> aware. There's a great depth of consciousness and they do fun,
> but powerful, ceremonies. A few years ago we built a huge
> stone circle there with a well, what we call a 'well of light'
> in the centre, which is a ritual circle aligned to the planetary
> directions, and it holds 300 people. So they're dedicated and
> serious at Fairy Congress whilst also having a lot of fun."
>
> R. J. Stewart in an interview with Emily Carding, 2011

· · · · · · ·

The Fairy and Human Relations Congress is an outdoor event that has a highly spiritual focus without losing sight of its sense of fun. This weekend of magickal workshops and family entertainment has been held annually in the remote and beautiful location of Twisp in the Pacific Northwest, its purpose being communication and cooperation with the realm of Faery. Though it can be something of a pilgrimage to get there, it is well worth the trip for those not drawn to the more commercial and entertainment-oriented events. For more information, please visit www.fairycongress.com.

Europe

Elf Fantasy Fair

The largest and most popular Faery community event in mainland Europe is undoubtedly the annual Elf Fantasy Fair. People travel from all over the world to the Netherlands to show their most ostentatious Faery finery at this outdoor weekend event. There is usually also a large selection of musical entertainment and more of an adult focus than other festival events. For more information, please visit www.haarzuilens .elffantasyfair.com.

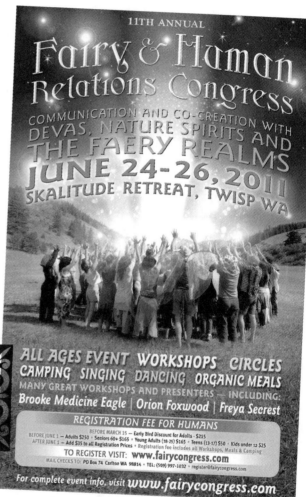

LEFT: image courtesy
of Karen Kay; RIGHT:
image courtesy of Jan Kinsey

UK

KAREN KAY'S FAERY EVENTS

Karen Kay is the undisputed queen of the UK's Faery scene, with a full year of top-quality Faery festivals, fairs, and balls! Artists and musicians from all over the world come to perform at her events, which include the Avalon Faery Ball, which takes place three times a year; the Avalon Faery Fayre, an indoor faery market that takes place three times a year in Glastonbury to coincide with the Avalon Faery Ball; and the biggest outdoor event of its kind in the UK: Three Wishes Faery Fest, a family-oriented event packed full of vendors, entertainers, and workshops in the beautiful Cornish countryside.

Karen Kay and friend

Karen Kay is also the editor of the highly popular magazine *Faeries and Enchantment* (FAE) and its sister publication *Mermaids and Mythology*. Here she shares some insight into how the events first came about and why Faery is so important to her life and work. For more information, please visit www.faeryevents.com.

An Interview with Karen Kay

Which came first, the events or FAE magazine?

I'VE BEEN ORGANISING events since 1994, and they were holistic events, mystic fayres. Then in 2004 I was inspired to do a faerie, angels, and healing fayre, which was the first time faeries came into the events for me. Getting the Faery element into the event was quite challenging, as I found that all the Faery people were quite shy and not coming forward. I'd been writing to Brian Froud for a couple of years with no success, and someone said "Oh, Brian's in Truro doing a book signing." I found myself at the front of the queue, and I was able to invite him to come. He was really friendly, and it was a really interesting conversation. From that he came to the first Faery Ball in 2006. Because he was there, everyone wanted to be there, and everyone came out of the woodwork! It was fantastic!

I'd heard there was an American magazine about faeries (*Fairies Magazine*), and it seemed a natural progression for me to do a magazine about faeries. It was an evolution, once I saw the interest there was. I didn't know it was going to go worldwide and be as popular as it was!

How did you have the idea to start an outdoor Faery Festival?

THE FIRST FESTIVAL was in 2007. I remember I was really strongly guided that there needed to be an event, an outdoor event. A celebration that was non-religious, you didn't have to be Pagan or any-

thing like that. Anyone, at any level of understanding, who loved faeries could come along. I didn't know what to call it...and I was hanging some washing on the line when I saw this dandelion seed head. The lawn had been cut, and I remember thinking, "How has that dandelion survived when everything else has been cut?" Then three of the little seeds flew up, one, two, three, and then the idea of "three wishes" came into my head. Three Wishes Faery Fest. I knew what it had to be called, I knew it had to exist.

I also knew through guidance that it had to be at midsummer. Then I was prompted to announce it even though I had no idea where it was going to be! I was being tested, my faith and trust. I knew it would be in Cornwall, but not where it would be. Then I was led to the venue, and the owner was crazy enough to say, "Let's do it!"

Why are the Faery events so important?

IT'S A CELEBRATION of Faery as real energies, the guardians of the earth. They really are connected to earth very strongly, and without them, I don't think the earth would survive. It's a very intrinsic thing. The festival is to create a utopia for a few days where people can come and feel really safe with likeminded people and just have a party. Dress up and have fun! It's wonderful, because it's creative, it's innocent. All your cares can go and you can just be in a beautiful location and celebrate faeries.

And when you think about faeries, whether consciously or unconsciously, then ultimately it will bring you back to the environment. That's why I think the faeries want us to do these events, to bring attention back to the land and to faeries as the guardians of the land. We really need to look after our planet, and without sounding like an eco-warrior type, it's that—with wings and a bit of sparkle!

Faces of Faery

Let's take a journey in pictures through some Faery events and see the different ways people express their love for Faery…

Here I am (CENTER) in full bling mode with author
Kim Huggens (LEFT) and artist Esther Remmington (RIGHT)

Naomi von Monsta (TOP RIGHT) and artist Liselotte Eriksson
(ABOVE) have opted for a deliciously dark yet colourful look,
bringing a touch of Goth to their Faery costumes. Note the
wonderful details such as the skull headdress!

Artist Jennie Cooper combines
a pair of horns with lavender
and innocent white to create
a playful look.

There is always a frolicking faun
or two to be found at a good Faery
festival! Here, the furry legs, horns,
and hoofiness are provided by
restaurant owner Darren Williams.

BELOW: Alison Spence attended the Mermaids
and Pirates Ball as a rather wonderful sea witch.
RIGHT: Bryony Whistlecraft's natural elfin beauty
is enhanced by a tasteful pair of antlers.
(photo courtesy of www.tpftpf.com)

Felicity Fyr Le Fay and my daughter, Willow, lead the faerie procession through the grounds of the 2011 Three Wishes Faery Fest in Cornwall.

LEFT: Musician Abigail Seabrook
looks beautiful in gentle pastel colours, wings,
flowers, and glitter. BELOW: Leaf reads tarot
and oracle cards at Faery events.

LEFT: Faery entertainer Trixie Pixie happily shows off her fiery outfit—corset and tutu, always a winning combination! BELOW: A wandering gypsy caravan sells beautiful carvings of Faery fungus.

"As with inspiration, once you know where to find it, it is everywhere! My work is an expression of my world, of which I feel is neither completely in everyday reality nor completely in Faery…I have attempted to express through texture, colour, personality, emotion, and character. With all my sculptures I feel new emotions, as if they have grown from within me. I hope that the creatures who have been expressed from my world bring something new to everyone… but, strangely, you may feel as if you have already met!"

Armorel Hamilton
(www.armorelhamilton.com)

• • • • • • •

LEFT: Artist Armorel Hamilton at her stall at one of the Avalon Faery Fayres. ABOVE: Artist Linda Ravenscroft sketches one of her fans.

"I just love making beautiful things. I've always made things since I was tiny and just want to spread the magic, to bring it back into people's lives. My sources of inspiration come from folklore and nature; one stems from the other. I want to try and bring the beauty back so that people can see—be inspired by nature—and know that we don't all have to live in a concrete jungle."

Chyna de la Mer
(www.tangleheads.co.uk)

• • • • • • •

Faery events always have unique handmade arts and crafts for sale, such as the beautiful things on offer from craftsperson Chyna de la Mer.

The lovely Tamara Newman is one of many talented,
glamorous artists emerging on the Faery scene.

There is always a wide choice of entertainment
for children in the daytime…

LEFT: ...and for adults at nightime!
ABOVE: Also for the adults, there are all manner
of magical potions available at the bar.

Flame by name, flame by nature!
(photo courtesy of TPF Images and Arts,
www.tpftpf.com)

ABOVE: Felicity Fyr Le Fay and my daughter, Willow.
RIGHT: Aspiring artist and children's author Natalee
          May is clearly an elf—no question!

ABOVE: Artist Laura Daligan's love of mythology shows itself in her serpentine choice of costume for the Faery Ball! Medussssssssssaaaa… RIGHT: The mighty Kim Huggens, esoteric author, takes on the Faery Ball as an awesome tribal Faery warrior! (Photo courtesy of Nic Philips)

ABOVE: Kathryn Kerr has created a delightful peacock-inspired outfit with fascinating peacock feather eyebrows! RIGHT: Many people love the creative challenge of making their own Faery outfits, such as fifteen-year-old Cara Jones, who created this stunning ensemble with the help of her mother. OPPOSITE PAGE: Juliet Prentice identifies with the spirits of the sea in this glorious mermaid costume that creatively incorporates her wheelchair. But she has been caught by a fierce pirate! (He'd better watch out… mermaids bite.)

Unicorn Faerie FaeNix dances
beautifully with her Isis wings.

LEFT: Faery festivals often incorporate theatrical performances. Here, actor Matthew Wade makes a dashing Oberon, the Faery King, in Shakespeare's *A Midsummer Night's Dream* (photo courtesy of Oliver McNeil, www.legend-photography.com). RIGHT: Helen Robinson shows us that pirates are a force to be reckoned with (photo and pirate costume courtesy of TPF images and arts, www.tpftpf.com).

Don't forget to buy a new pair of wings from
Twisted Twinkle before you go!

The Depth Behind the Glitter...

One of the many people who provide a bit of sparkle to Faery events—or, more accurately, a great bucket-load of sparkle—is the glamorous Felicity Fyr Le Fay, a circus performer and entertainer from New Zealand who now lives and works in the UK as well as travels around the world teaching about Faery through entertainment. Here she gives a very personal and fascinating insight into the depth behind the sparkle, about the difficulties of growing up in New Zealand without a community of like-minded people, and why the festivals and events give a much-needed clan identity to those who may always have felt different or lonely because of their identification with Faery.

There is a lot of Faery energy in New Zealand, and the mythology is predominantly Maori, where there is a lot of Faery lore...they have giants, they have a kind of dragon, and they have the Faery people, who are very similar to the Tuatha de Danann. They have red hair, they're very tall, ethereal, and godlike. But when I was growing up, New Zealand was not at the point culturally where Maori lore was being taught in schools, and so I didn't know anything about it, though I did read British mythology. I do believe that when the British came over to New Zealand they brought the faeries with them, especially with the trees and foreign flora that was brought there.

So as a child there was a lot of magic around but no one to talk to about it at all. I felt really lonely, really sad, I was the funny-looking girl at school who got picked on. I was very obviously different and I didn't fit in. This is really common with Faery people: we're very passionate and sensitive, and we feel everything so intensely. We feel the environment pouring through our souls, we feel the pain in the trees and the suffering of animals. We can relate to and connect with animals, but when talking to other humans we're sometimes confused because there are so many façades. Faery children find that confusing—they're not used to all the human layers, not having experienced them in their previous incarnations.

It was really difficult for me, especially after the age of about ten. Before that I told everyone, all my family, about being a faerie—I would have exquisitely vivid dreams about going to Faeryland and my experiences there and all of a sudden, when I was ten, it wasn't cool anymore. All your friends are being cool and suave and hanging out at the mall, trying to smoke and all that. This girl whose mind was full of unicorns and magic and who would get lost in the woods following the sound of bells just didn't fit in.

I decided the thing for me to do was to look inwards and learn from nature, so I became a Pagan before I knew anything about what a Pagan was. I went through a phase where I read about every religion I could get my hands on. When I read about Druidry and Wicca, I realised that it was everything I had worked out entirely for myself. It was truth that I had found for myself. There were no books about Faery specifically, but I realised that if these other things I had discovered were true, then the part of me that was Faery was also true.

There's a lot of different kinds of entertaining that I do, and children's birthday parties are the most important. Every once in a while there comes along one or two of these children, and you can see they're Faery people too. When you're talking about the environment, about being called somewhere and getting lost in the woods, you can see that it's happened to them too. Not just those children, but all the children—you're trying to give them as much magic and beauty that they can hold in their souls so that as they're growing up in a world that throws tax and paperwork and all this ridiculousness that throws life into a tangle, they have this beautiful place inside of them that gives them strength so that they can become the powerful tree of a person that they are meant to be. It's so important for people to know that if you want to go out into the world and make it better, you can do that, with the full backing of the otherworld behind you.

"With all people, when they see beauty—real beauty, not
necessarily pretty but something that makes them passionately
feel—it's something that imprints on their mind more
powerfully than any image. So if you want to pass on a
message about healing, about the environment, about helping
the animal kingdom, the most powerful way you can pass
that message on is by doing a performance that hits them
right in the heart chakra. So that's what I try to do."

Felicity Fyr Le Fay

• • • • • • •

Images courtesy of Steve Williams
(www.stevewilliamsphoto.com)

The Mermaids

Just as Faery is growing in popularity as part of the growing urgency of environmental awareness, so mermaids are also growing in popularity, even with their own events, such as Mer-Con in Las Vegas, the world's first mermaid convention. The attendees of this event are a phenomenon in themselves, the closest thing you'll likely find in physical reality to real mermaids, and many of them believe they are truly merfolk in human incarnations. These mermaids have specially made tails that they can wear underwater and often hold impressive records for holding their breath in order to perform. One such mermaid is the extraordinary performer Mermaid Melissa, who dons her mermaid guise in order to raise awareness of the world's oceans and their importance to the future of the world. For more information, visit www.mermaidmelissa.com.

Image courtesy of Jessica Yakamna
(www.dropjawphotography.com)

Creative Challenge: Faery on a Budget

A common issue that arises is that people would like to come to festivals and other Faery events but are unsure of what to wear or feel they can't afford the amazing outfits that they see others wearing. It's true that there are some fantastic specialist craftspeople making high-quality items of clothing just for this market, but it is also true that a lot of people make their own costumes and piece them together from carefully sourced bargains. I feel it is also important to emphasise that plenty of people have a wonderful time at festivals without having to dress up, but if you do want to try a creative approach, here are a few ideas that you don't need to be in any way skilled to be able to achieve.

With a small budget and eco-friendly principles of reusing materials in mind, I set myself the challenge of putting together a complete outfit in a day.

All images on pages 216–237 by
Studio Lotus (www.studiolotus.co.uk)

A friend and I set off into a local town hoping to achieve our mission of a Faery outfit on a budget.

We decided that charity shops were a great option, for not only would we be recycling materials but we should be able to find easily adaptable fabric and clothing at affordable prices. Plus all the money we spent would be going to good causes—bonus!

It can be difficult finding suitable items in the right size, but persistence and a bit of imagination can reap great rewards. We found a purple skirt and a glittery purple top in one shop. The top was rather large, but we had some ideas about easy ways to alter it with no sewing needed. The skirt was a little plain, but again, creative ideas were starting to brew…

Since the top and skirt would obviously form the main part of the outfit, we now needed to accessorise to achieve our desired effect. After much trawling through further charity shops we found a perfect necklace for a tiny amount.

We resorted to a local fancy dress shop to find a very affordable mask and a pair of rainbow-coloured fishnet tights.

We then needed to think about wings, of course. For this we returned to the charity shops and decided that a pair of net curtains could be adapted in some creative ways to make a fun winglike cloak. We also spotted a silver belt and a metallic scarf that gave us some more interesting ideas.

Pleased with our purchases, we returned home and started to create the costume.

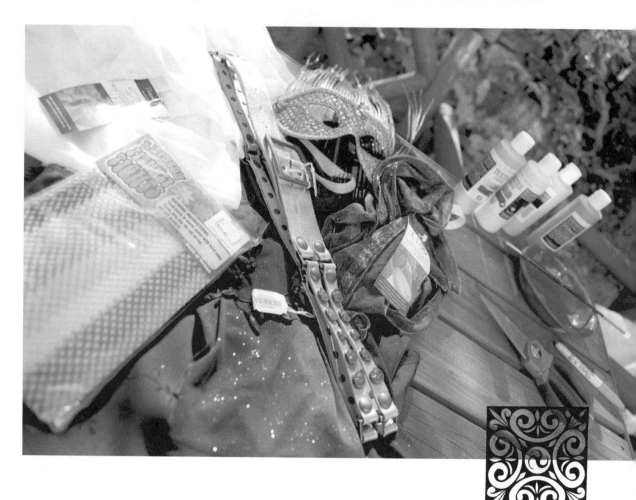

The ill-fitting top we adapted by cutting a series of parallel holes down its back and using a long, thin strip of one of the net curtains as a ribbon. This managed to create a corsetlike effect that gathered the material and made the top a better fit.

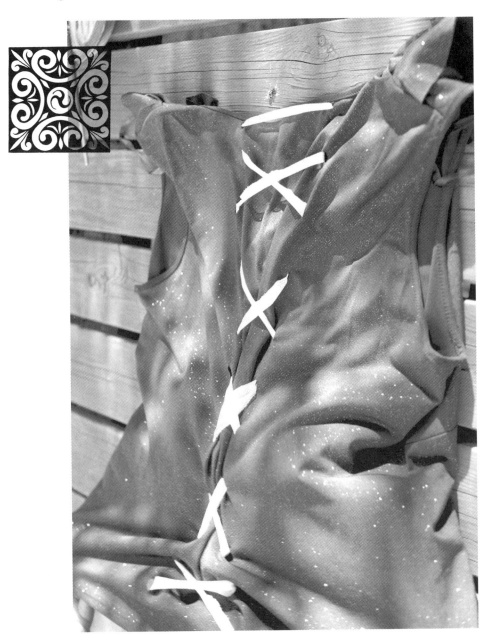

The skirt was in two layers, so the top layer we cut simply into petal-shaped flaps to give it more of an organic effect.

The silver belt and one of the net curtains were put to good use. The curtain was cut into long strips that were then tied to the belt to make a rag skirt. This is a really easy and effective use of any scrap material you might have around the home. If you have the time, you could also dye it different colours.

The other curtain became the wings. With one long cut up the middle, then two strips cut next to that to use as neckties, it was just a question of cutting out winglike shapes on each side, with a little hole in each corner for a finger to fit through. Again, this could be dyed or painted if you have the time. Even marker pens can be used to good effect to add some colour!

With the addition of the rainbow tights and glitter mask, the outfit was complete. You *shall* go to the ball!

This entire outfit cost only £25 and took just a couple of hours to put together. If you have a bit more time to find the really good bargains and put in a personal, creative touch, you too can create something truly unique and amazing!

The Power of Dressing Up

It is easy to dismiss the idea of dressing up as frivolous or as something that is "just for fun" and quite separate from any genuine connection or magickal practice. Indeed, it can be just that, and it is, of course, not in any way a required part of Faery Craft if it is something that simply does not sit well with you. However, hidden beneath the face paint and extravagant clothing there are depths to explore that yield surprising results and even practical everyday applications.

This may seem like a superficial concept until we consider the fact that ceremonial magick of invocation and classical theatre have the same roots, and that by taking on the appearance of the gods, usually through masks, actors would become more priest than player, taking on some part of that divine quality for the span of a play. Indeed, masks are still widely used within both theatre and magick, and as both a trained actor and a practitioner of magick, I can confirm that the effect in both cases is extremely powerful. Masks are fascinating objects with a power and personality of their own, which even without intent can affect the energy and behaviour of the wearer almost immediately. How, then, is putting on a costume or dressing with intent any different? Wearing face paint or particular makeup is a form of mask work and can be just as effective. In fact, if we consider the potency of energy contained within a painting done with magickal intent and then consider how that would affect an individual acting, in a way, as a living canvas, how could it not be transformative? When we combine this with the idea of forming an entire costume with this intent, we have a powerful technique that can also be a great deal of fun!

We have already seen how many people use dressing up at balls and festivals as a way of expressing their inner selves or to simply rejoice in the beauty of imagination. Let us now consider how we can harness the art of dressing up as a magickal technique for deepening our understanding and connection, and for bringing our inner elemental energies into balance.

EXERCISE: Dressing as the Elements

This is not a clearly instructed exercise as such but is more of a series of suggestions for you to try if you wish, as well as a commentary on the effects that I and others experienced whilst experimenting with these ideas ourselves. We have already taken an in-depth look at the elements and worked towards connecting with the different aspects of each element through contemplation. For the most part this is a passive, receptive process, connecting to our surroundings through opening our awareness and expanding our energy to join with the landscape. This results in a powerful internal process that can lead to understanding and transformative wisdom when performed regularly and with the right intent. However, let us also consider another approach that may be tried alongside these spiritual techniques. Why not transform the physical appearance in order to take on the qualities of each element?

Air

Traditionally the element of air is associated with the colours yellow, gold, and white, so you may wish to use any or all of these colours in combination for your air costume. Depending on how much of a hoarder you are, you may well find you already have things that you can use or adapt for this purpose. Also think about using makeup, face paint, or even a mask; changing your facial appearance is probably the most important part of this technique, as for the most part it is your face that transmits your personality to the world around you—it is the window to your emotions and inner thoughts. When we change that outer appearance, the most remarkable inner processes can occur! We chose to use face paint in white, silver, and gold. You do not need to be an expert to create really good effects with face paint. Here is a basic step-by-step guide.

You will need:

* At least two or three colours in decent quality water-based face paints that will blend well together.

* Makeup sponges. In fact, we used a cut-up dishwashing sponge for this exercise (unused, obviously)!

* Brushes, at least one thicker and one for fine detail. There are special face-painting brushes available, but we just used regular artist's paintbrushes, and they work great!

* A bowl or cup of clean water.

* A cloth or paper towel for blotting any excess water.

Step One

Using a damp sponge (be sure that it is not too wet, blotting any excess water if necessary), apply your foundation colour around the eyes, nose, and cheeks, including part of the forehead if you wish. In this case we used white as a foundation, a good all-purpose base colour that will help other colours to stand out, and of course very appropriate for air!

Step Two

Again using the sponge, choose another colour to bring out highlights and/or lowlights. Here we used gold around the eyes and cheeks, with a bit of silver to bring out the cheekbones. It seemed fitting for the element of air to try and sharpen the features, emphasizing bone structure.

Step Three

Using the brushes, add any details in a colour that will stand out against your foundation. In this case, a masklike effect was created using a stronger density of white over the gold, and a fine brush was used to create some dots and to emphasize the eyebrows.

Step Four

Consider a complementary lip colour. You can use lipstick, but we chose to use the same colours of face paint, again using white as a foundation and then gold over the top.

Step Five

Look fabulous!

You may, of course, decide that you would rather use a mask to transform your facial appearance. In the case of the element of air, any birdlike or feathered mask would be an obvious choice, or perhaps a simple metallic gold half-mask.

Wigs are also wonderfully transformative and don't need to be expensive. For the element of air I chose a rather punky white wig that I've had for more years than I care to think of, and I'm so glad I kept hold of it as it turned out to be quite perfect for this exercise. I also found a peacock feather fascinator to wear over the wig.

For the clothing, choose something that you perhaps wouldn't normally wear, or at least wear them in unusual ways, and think about the colours and qualities of the element. I chose a striking gold dress that I picked up as a bargain from a bellydance hafla, along with a white and gold bellydance belt. This had the added benefit of adding an auditory dimension to my ensemble! You may prefer something simpler, perhaps something floaty that catches every breeze or something classical that brings to mind the great thinkers of the ancient world. Of course, for the element of air, wings are a great accessory. The wings I am wearing in this picture are effective yet extremely simple in construction, made from iridescent cellophane and coathanger wire. Feathered wings would be another good choice, or perhaps a billowing cloak or Isis wings such as are used in belly dancing. You may also notice that I chose to use a representative tool for the element of air as a prop—in this case, a rather fine dagger.

You might wear this costume for an event, but I also recommend trying this as an exercise out in nature, perhaps with a small group of friends, not only so that you don't feel too self-conscious and there is an element of fun, but also so that you can observe any changes in each other's energy and behaviour. Try to find a place where you won't be pestered by passersby and where you can experience the element of air directly.

How do you feel? Are you thinking, acting, or talking any differently? How is your understanding of the element affected?

Fire

Red is the elemental colour for fire, but any combination of shades of red, orange, and gold will help to bring out those fiery qualities! These colours should also be used in your makeup, mask, or face paint. Bearing these colours in mind, follow the four steps as listed for the element of air. Here I used a gold base with the sponge and a masklike phoenix design painted on in red. Fire is the element of passion and action, so try to build those qualities into your costume. I chose a very tribal-style belly dance costume, with lots of red and gold that reflected the light and layers that moved with my body. You should choose something that you can move in freely that makes you feel confident and powerful. Since my hair is currently blond and red, I did not use a wig for this element but instead used a lot of hairspray to create a flamelike style. Having exponentially increased my flammability by doing so, I kept a safe distance from the fire!

I also found the effect was enhanced once more by the addition of a tool for a prop. In this case I used a staff with bells attached and found myself wielding it like a warrior! Well, posing like a wannabe warrior actually…

Fire would be a great choice of elemental costume for any Faery ball or festival, as it is bound to bring out your inner party demon! Again, I encourage you to try this as a magickal exercise also, with a small group of friends around a fire, and note any changes in mood, energy, and behaviour.

Water

Blue is the colour most associated with water, and it is nicely complemented by white and silver, as well as some shades of green and turquoise. Clothes for this element could be either free and flowing or clingy and glistening like the scales of a fish. I chose a Grecian-style white dress that I had borrowed and never returned from my college's theatre wardrobe department fifteen years ago. At the time it was the costume for Lady Macbeth, whom I, as an evil director, made walk into a cold and rather dank pond for her final scene. It seemed only fitting that I should now wear it for the element of water and take it for another dip! Over this I wore a pale blue organza veil for a very classical look.

The blue curly wig was less classical, of course, but along with the silver and blue face paint did serve to transform my appearance to the extent that I was unrecognisable.

If you want to achieve this look with face paint, use moonlike colours as a base—say, white and grey or silver if you have it. Then add detail and spirals around the eyes and cheekbones. It's simple yet effective!

We used a silver chalice, which is the ritual and symbolic magical tool for the element of water. It was entrancing scooping up water and pouring it back out, watching the light reflecting from the droplets as they fell and hearing the song they made as they returned to the flowing river.

Being able to stand in the river whilst dressed as a creature of that element brought feelings of tranquillity and an awareness of deep inner compassion, despite posing for the photographs whilst knee-deep in water.

Remember to try this out near or in the element if you can, and note any changes in your usual thought patterns, behaviour, or general character.

Water and Earth meet at the shore

Earth

For the element of earth I experimented on a willing victim, my friend Anna Simon. Despite the fact that she did not choose any of her costume herself and believed that she was merely dressing up in order to pose for photographs, she found it to be a profoundly transformative experience. Indeed, both the photographer and I found the change in her energy and behaviour to be quite remarkable, noticing a real connection between her and her surroundings, particularly the trees, and a deep sensuality, confidence, and grace.

In Anna's own words:

> We headed to the woods, and as we walked down the hill and the great old trees rose up before us, I joked about being in my "element" (or, in fact, being in myself, ha ha), but once inside the boundary of green, I have to admit my perception was already changing. I've always had an appreciation for nature, for spaces untouched by humankind. It isn't terribly out of my character to randomly hug or even sing to trees, so this wasn't a massive shift in perception. But something did occur that afternoon, despite the itchiness of the wig and the weight of the cloak. I connected with earth—I daresay I even became earth, just for a little while.
>
> As I posed for the camera with an apple in hand, I felt that if you looked away, you'd turn around and I'd have blended into the scenery. What a strange feeling to mesh into one's surroundings on an emotional level but not feel lonely or outcast. I walked taller, more elegantly (save for a little skirmish with my skirt getting caught in sticky bushes), and felt a peace I have longed for. The icing on the cake came after Emily had finished her water session and we were walking back; our photographer and great friend Steve was seeing a great shot of me next to a tree, and when I approached that tree I felt like I was wrapping my arms around a handsome, earthy man! Everywhere I looked, the trees were more vivid, the air was sweeter, and the area seemed to welcome me like an old friend.

Here's what we did. The main colour for earth is, of course, green, but all earthy tones of brown and even black are suitable, or even autumnal hues of rusty reds. Again, I used face paint, this time using the sponge to create a foundation of green, then darker areas

"How is it that I connected so deeply with my surroundings without so much as intent to do so? I've always struggled with meditation, and I'm terrible at grounding myself to the extent of clumsiness; I walk into doors and walls constantly. So for me to suddenly snap my roots on, that was a soul-opening feeling."

Anna

· · · · · · ·

with black around the eyes. Leafy details were then drawn in black and green with a brush, the whole face taking about five minutes to render, yet with very dramatic effect. As you may have noticed by now, I have a small collection of wigs at my disposal, and I chose a very natural long brown wig for Anna's look, complemented by an ivy headdress that very simply consists of a piece of fake vine wrapped around her head as a crown— so effective and very easy to do!

I also found a long green skirt that worked perfectly with the plain black tunic that she was already wearing, and finished the look off with my rather heavy outdoor cloak, which is a beautiful shade of forest green and keeps out all weathers! Consider what aspects of earth you wish to emphasise in your costume. For fertility you might choose brighter green hues; for stability you might choose browns and blacks. You might even want to try shades of grey if you are trying to strengthen your connection with spirits of stone. If you wanted to try a mask, why not make one yourself? There are plenty of blank templates available that you can paint and add to with papier-mâché or perhaps feathers and plastic foliage. Horned or antlered headdresses are also a nice idea as ways to express or encourage connection to this element.

Practical Everyday Applications

Once you have fully immersed yourself in each of the elements in this way, you can draw on your fresh understanding and the memory of any energetic shift whenever you wish, without the need to dress up to such an extreme. You can also apply the same technique on a much more subtle basis in your everyday life, particularly through conscious use of colour symbolism. For example, for increased confidence and drive, you may wish to draw on the power of fire by wearing an item of red clothing, perhaps altering your makeup or even colouring your hair in a red tone. To emphasise logical thinking and clear communication, try consciously wearing something yellow or gold, or perhaps a subtle piece of feathered jewellery, for the element of air. To bring a feeling of inner peace and bring forth the compassionate side of your nature, try wearing the colours of water, such as calming shades of blue and turquoise. Earthy colours such as green and brown will help to bring a feeling of grounded stability and connection with the natural world. You can also extend this idea further by looking at planetary attributions.

SUN: gold, yellow, orange; success, confidence, charisma, happiness

MOON: white, silver; mystery, magick, intuition, dreams

MARS: red; power, strength, status, sex

VENUS: green; femininity, love, beauty, fertility

MERCURY: light blue; communication, thought, travel

JUPITER: purple, dark blue; expansion, hope, joy, luck

SATURN: brown, black; structure, organisation, time, law

As you can see, with this awareness you have a whole palette of tools at your disposal to bring energies into your life and to encourage conscious connection with the world around you. The art of dressing with intent is a very Faery kind of magick, for just like the wonders of the spirit within the land, it goes unnoticed in plain view.

Suggested Activities

Practice

Dress with intent and awareness—it doesn't need to be conspicuous. Make notes of how the different colours and styles affect your energy and what kind of attention or events you attract throughout the day.

Celebrate

Why not throw a fancy dress party for your friends with the four elements as a theme? You could also try preparing food and snacks with the elements and colours in mind!

Research

Find out if there are any Faery events or festivals within travelling distance, and make plans to attend. If not, do you feel ready to organise one yourself? Everyone starts somewhere, and you could bring great joy to others as well as yourself by spreading the awareness of Faery.

Create

Using a blank template (available from craft stores or online retailers), create a mask for the element that you feel the least connection with, putting thought into materials, colours, and techniques used. When it is finished, spend some time in contemplation of this element whilst wearing the mask, and see how your understanding expands. This should also help to bring valuable balance to your energies.

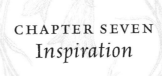

CHAPTER SEVEN
Inspiration

"O, then, I see Queen Mab hath been with you.
She is the fairies' midwife, and she comes
In shape no bigger than an agate-stone
On the fore-finger of an alderman,
Drawn with a team of little atomies
Athwart men's noses as they lie asleep…"

Shakespeare, *Romeo and Juliet*

· · · · · · ·

F aeries have long been associated with inspiration, though whether they climb into our noses as we sleep (as the great bard describes in the quote above) is debatable! Inspiration is the quality we gain from the south and the element of fire, but it may be found all around us, from the most epic landscape to the tiniest blade of grass. We should also never underestimate the power that we all have to inspire each other, and for this reason we should never be shy of creative undertakings, for though there will always be those whose will is to detract from our achievements, there will equally be those who are inspired by our own will to act on creative impulse.

This chapter is intended to help you find the sustenance of inspiration upon your path. There are many inspirational voices within the Faery community, and all offer their own perspectives, some of which will no doubt resonate on a personal level more than others, but all of which have something to offer. Walking a spiritual or magickal path can seem isolating at times, especially when those around us do not share our views, experiences, and beliefs. This is why in Faery Craft it is so valuable to know that there is a rich and varied community out there, full of creative, intelligent, and open people who share their gifts and teachings of inspiration with the world. You are not alone.

Faery Paths, Traditions, and Groups

Faery Craft does not require traditional initiation or membership in any group or religion, nor does it preclude such membership, as it can become part of any path that is wide enough to allow our Faery allies to walk by our side. Naturally, a number of groups and traditions have formed over the years that have particular connection to Faery, so we shall look some of the more prominent and intriguing ones here.

The Faery Tradition and R. J. Stewart

There is strong vein of Faery lore and practices that until modern times was passed down orally through tales and folklore. Although the oral tradition has all but faded into the mists, there are resources and teachers who can point the way to not only reclaiming the hidden wisdom inherent in the lore but finding the living and evolving tradition within it that is just as relevant now, if not more so, than it was to our ancestors. One of the most respected teachers of this tradition is the Scottish author, esotericist, and musician R. J. Stewart. He currently has forty books in publication and dedicates a great deal of time and energy to teaching magickal arts and Faery tradition to groups both in the United States and Europe. I was lucky enough to be able to visit him in his home in Glastonbury, England, and gain insight into his perspective and experience of the Faery realm.

> *Was there an experience that stands out in your mind as being your first truly otherworldly experience with the Faery realm or like an initiatory experience that came from them as opposed to from other people?*

Well, there's several. I had lots of experiences on sacred sites in Britain, really from the early 1970s onwards, and then around 1980 I visited Robert Kirk's Faery hill in Scotland, and as a result of my experiences there I produced a new edition of his famous book *The Secret Commonwealth*, which is about Scottish Faery tradition, and I wrote a commentary on it. You know, I had a lot of spiritual experiences when I was at Kirk's Faery hill, as have many other people. It is a powerful place.

Are there any that you can talk about, or is it all very secret?

Well, that's more difficult. What happens with the Faery traditions is the more willing people are to talk about it, the less they've experienced, and the less willing they are to talk about it, the more they've experienced, which makes it very difficult. You find the same thing hidden within the interviews noted by W. Y. Evans-Wentz, the famous scholar who wrote *The Faery-Faith in Celtic Countries*. He didn't speak Irish and he went round interviewing the Irish grandmothers and grandfathers and country people generally, and often he had to go with the local Catholic priest, so he's not going to get proper answers to his questions. He'd ask them, "Did you ever see fairies?" and they'd say, "No, never seen any. But my uncle used to see them, it was a long time ago, and they were very small." And that means, "I see them every day, and they're really big." There is also something inherent in the Irish language that is difficult for modern English people to understand, for things are often referred to as their opposite in Gaelic. Thus "the little people" actually meant "the big people." This has been forgotten.

What do you think the most important qualities are for someone who wants to seriously work with Faery?

You have to be very honest, because they sense all deception; you can't hide anything from them. One of the early writings about the Faery realm is that you have to go there without a shadow on your heart, because if you have a shadow on your heart, they'll tear you to pieces. But if your heart is pure, they're already your friends, and they will love you. So that's the old-fashioned way of saying what we would say today—that you have to have integrity, and you have to be truthful and honest, like every fairy tale! In every fairy tale it's the person who is truthful and honest who does well, and the person who's deceitful and selfish does very badly.

You have to have a sense of humour, because they're very humorous and they make jokes all the time and do all sorts of strange things. And you have to be patient, because some Faery things are very instant, and others take a long, long time.

R. J. Stewart

What would you say are the big things to avoid when working with Faery?

Avoid being superior, and avoid thinking of faeries as "little helpers," and always be respectful. Respect goes a long, long way. Never, ever assume that they will do anything for you, anything at all, because even if they've done something for you for years, one day they'll say, "No, we've never done that…we're not going to do that for you." So never assume anything. Always expect the unexpected!

*How important do you think place is—being rooted
in a place for connecting with Faery?*

I think it's very important. There are some things to do with Faery magick that you can do anywhere—anywhere in the world, it doesn't matter. But there are other things that you can only do when you're tuned in to one place and tuned in to that place relatively long-term. So I think place is extremely important. And you know that's true in human life, too. There are people who never leave their hometown and there are people who travel all over the place, and the Faery beings are just like human beings in that respect.

*What would you say the difference is, then, between the kinds of beings
who are able to travel with you and those who are tied to a locality?*

This is where it gets interesting, and not enough is known or taught about this due to lack of practical experience in our alternative communities at this time. Especially because there's a lot of assumptions about what Faery beings are and statements are made about them without really trying to relate to them and come into a proper understanding. Certain Faery beings can move around freely and really have a great sort of independence of energy. Others are closely tied to springs or wells or hills or forests and they can't move around freely, even if they're powerful. And so those are two of the quite clear distinctions that you have—the ones that can move freely anywhere and the ones that are really in a location. And really we have to try to understand both.

*I've heard from people where they have experienced beings who are clearly
deeply connected to the land but seem to take on some qualities of their
appearance from the people who had moved to that place from other areas—
for example, faeries of Celtic appearance have been encountered in some
areas of Canada. Is it that they travelled over with the people or that the
people seeing them are perceiving them through some sort of filter?*

I think it's a mixture of all of these things. Irish mystic AE (real name George William Russell) was actually interviewed by Evans-Wentz anonymously, and he also wrote in his autobiography, which is called *The Candle of Vision*, that when he was out in the remote parts of Western Ireland, the Faery beings would appear as lights. They looked like oval shapes made of light in the remote places. But when they got closer to human habitation they started to look more like human beings.

This is significant because they take a form, a visual presentation, from the human memory and from the human imagination. And guess what? They're always several hundred years out of date. This is why a lot of people think of faeries as looking medieval or sometimes they appear in eighteenth-century costumes. They tend to draw, for some reason, from the collective memory but appear to be several hundred years behind the times. You don't see them dressed up in the latest Gucci outfits!

*Something that is mentioned in Evans-Wentz and also much more
recently in John Matthews's channelled work,* The Sidhe, *is that a
time is coming when Faery beings will rise to the surface and be seen
again by all. Is that something that you see coming in the future?*

I think that it's a very important idea, and if humanity is going to *not* destroy itself, we need to come back to this heightened awareness of the spiritual dimensions of the Faery realm. I think that if we're going to go for something like that, it may take a while for it to happen; I don't think it's going to happen quickly, and it really depends on individuals and groups working at it to open it out. So it's all down to what we do—what we actually do.

There seems to be a number of people within the modern Faery community who
believe that they are faeries in human form. What do you think about that?

Well, I don't see why they shouldn't be! Why not? One of my teachers, Roberta Gray, who was an astrologer and very knowledgeable in Celtic tradition, used to say—she said this in the late 1960s/early '70s—that there were more and more beings being born into human bodies that had not been human before. That was very interesting, because she was saying that in the late 1960s, before the New Age movement, before any of the stuff we're so familiar with today, so that gave it a unique authenticity. It wasn't just a cool "something" that was around in a book. So I think it's very possible.

What do you see the future of Faery tradition being? Do you think
practitioners will always be in the minority or do you think it
will be more respected and known about in the future?

I don't know, I think there are multiple answers to that question. If, for example, our modernist culture breaks down and people start to live in new ways—like new versions of old or ancestral ways, I suppose—then we would see quite a widespread return to relating to the Faery beings and nature spirits, because it's clear, from tradition, that our ancestors regarded that as essential to survival. If our modernist culture doesn't break down, and we get more and more attuned to computers and cyber-networks and machines, then we'll continue to lose that awareness until eventually we lose it altogether. So I suppose the answer is we've got to find a middle ground somewhere between those two and hope that the culture doesn't break down but that people do become increasingly aware. Again, for me, the key is the environmental movement, because that's what makes people more aware of the spiritual worlds of nature.

So perhaps it will be the increasing connection with Faery that
will stop the breakdown from having to happen?

That's a very interesting point, yes, I think there's a lot of wisdom in that.

For more information, visit www.rjstewart.net.

John and Caitlín Matthews
(photo by Mark Brome)

Celtic Shamanism and John and Caitlín Matthews

Celtic shamanism is a path that embraces the native spiritual practices of the British Isles, honouring the ancestors and spirits of the land. It appeals to those who are drawn to nature-based spirituality and trance techniques and wish to work with the spirits of the Celtic and British landscape or who are of British or Celtic descent. As such, interaction and connection with Faery beings and nature spirits forms an important part of this practice. Shamanism and shamanic techniques in all their forms have become very popular in recent years, and two of the most prolific and respected authors in this field are John and Caitlín Matthews, a husband and wife team who have between them penned over a hundred books on Celtic mythology, shamanism, and related subjects, as well as taught core spiritual practices all over the world. I spoke to them about their relationship with Faery and the use of shamanic practices to strengthen our connection with the unseen realms.

How important is interaction with the Faery realm within Celtic shamanism?

J: Shamanism works at the level of spirit, and spirit includes the Faery realm, so they are actually very close. I find that the Faery kind show up quite a lot in journey work, though, in a way I can't really describe, my own encounters with them happen in a different way to normal journeying.

C: All shamanic traditions interact with different kinds of spirits, but the hidden ones are part of every tradition in every country, not just in Britain and Ireland.

Our ancestral traditions are informed by Faery lore, music, and wisdom on every level: historically, in the written record as well as in the oral tradition. But it is an ongoing, living lore, not one that has been anthropologically filed and forgotten. Those pathways have not been lost, but every time we journey or meditate or pray, we make "paths through the wheatfield."

Whenever we come to the thresholds of place or time, we encounter the hidden ones. As the elder race to humans and our neighbours, Faeries and ourselves have encounters and relationships; sometimes these are not happy relationships—especially when we build upon land without consideration—and these upsets often need to be arbitrated shamanically, for they can have consequences upon our descendants.

How can we strengthen connection with the Faery realm?

C: To have a strong relationship with the hidden ones, we need to acknowledge our interdependence with all life forms and live accordingly: with prayer, consideration, and respect. These are the daily duties towards the Faery realms that everyone should have. For myself, the songs I receive from Faery and the offerings that I give make a pathway down which mutual understanding has grown. The Faery allies that work with me in my shamanic practice do so because we enjoy each other's society and understand that their hearth and my hearth are those of neighbours.

J: Journey work strengthens any links with the otherworld in whatever form or of whatever type. Depending a lot on the individual, some may get Faery contacts of their own accord, others may have to work harder at it—it is those who could find shamanism a good means to opening doors to the Faery realms.

What advice would you give to people who wish to work with Faery?

J: Don't! Half seriously, I would say if you do so, be wary of all kinds of strangeness and wonder. Your whole life can be turned upside down by these beings, who can be every bit as cruel as they are kind. Of all the inner beings I work with, the Faery folk are the most uncompromising and variable. They can really like you one day, then, apparently, dislike you the next.

C: Be aware that the hidden ones are not there to grant our wishes: any relationship that we have with them is wrought of faithfulness, honour, and respect. Like humans, faeries can be in many different conditions, so be discriminate and clear in your dealings, with exactly the same street wisdom you would use in daily life—just because I see a man on the street doesn't mean he's well disposed to me. It's exactly the same if you meditate or journey and see a faerie! Beware of acting out of human acquisitiveness and, above all, keep any promises or agreements that you make with them. Don't claim Faery powers you don't possess—these belong to the hidden ones, not to you!

And from you specifically, John, I'd love to hear how working
with the glyph has changed your perceptions of Faery.

J: The great glyph was a gift that really started me on this aspect of the work. It was the first "in" thing they showed me, and when I got to use it, it opened ways between our worlds that were more powerful and direct than any I had known before. I continue to use it, and it has become a constant part of the work I do with Faery beings. They tell me they are very happy that so many people are using it today and look forward to welcoming all who are of good intention to their world.

. . . .

For more information, visit www.hallowquest.org.uk.

Faery Wicca

Faery Wicca is sometimes found referring to covens and individuals practicing a version of the Wiccan tradition, both initiatory and noninitiatory, with a strong emphasis on Faery beings and elementals and usually within a Celtic or pseudo-Celtic framework. Wicca itself is a popular magickal tradition, which, though relatively modern, has its roots in the grimoires, folk magick, and practices of ancient Greece, Rome, and Egypt. There is a strong aspect of polarity and balance within this tradition, as Wiccans work with a God and a Goddess, often putting much emphasis on the Divine Feminine. Wicca involves working with the elements and their guardians, and encourages a deep respect for nature and her hidden dimensions, so to work closely with Faery within this tradition is a natural extension.

Radical Faeries

"We have been a separate people…drifting together in
a parallel existence, not always conscious of each other,
yet recognizing one another by eyelock when we meet
here and there as outcasts…Spirit-people in the service
to the Great Mother…Shamans…rhapsodes, poets and
playwrights, healers and nurturers…visionaries…rebels."

Harry Hay speaking at the Spiritual Conference
for Radical Faeries in 1979

· · · · · · ·

The Radical Faeries are more of a movement than a group or tradition, based very much around gay sexuality and the freedom of expression, as well as the love of nature and the spirit of the land. Their roots may be found in their first gathering, the Spiritual Conference for Radical Faeries, which was organised by Harry Hay and John Burnside in 1979 and has since grown massively in numbers and reputation. Members of

Lisa Hunt, "Lord of the Greenwood"
(www.lisahuntart.com,
reproduced with kind permission
of US Games Systems, Inc.)

the Radical Faeries place prime importance on the celebration of individuality and "gay spirit," defining themselves as a race and culture apart and freeing their "inner faerie." Radical Faeries embrace the word *queer* as part of their identity, covering both gay men and women as well as transgender and bisexual, seeking to be liberated from what they see as the constrictive expectations and regulations of a heterocentric society. Fey (as some members also call themselves) celebrate the Celtic Pagan festivals in accordance with the wheel of the year as popularised by Wiccan-influenced paths. They hold events and meetings all over the world, and a number have bought land in wild places, such as Faerie Camp Destiny in Vermont, in order to provide retreat centres for members to pursue their magickal and spiritual paths away from the rest of the world.

Otherkin, Elven Spirituality, and the Silver Elves

One of the most recent groups to emerge within the Faery community is that of the Otherkin movement. Not a tradition as such, people who call themselves Otherkin believe that they are nonhuman souls, most commonly of the Faery races but also of magickal creatures such as dragons or animals such as wolves, born into human bodies. Whilst a number of these cases can be put down to pure fantasy or a psychological need for escapism, there is reason to give credence to the possibility that nonhuman souls could be born into a human life, particularly if your belief system includes reincarnation. Many believe that these souls have elected a human life to help bring humanity into a new age of connection and understanding.

Though the Otherkin movement arose as recently as the 1990s, its origins lie a little further back, in 1970s California, with the first group of people who dared to publicly come out as being "other," practicing nature-based magick and embracing an elven identity as daughters (though they were both men and women) of the great Earth Goddess. I interviewed a magickal couple known as the Silver Elves, who discovered their own elven identities through contact with the Elf Queen's Daughters in the 1970s, as I wished to learn more of their fascinating way of life.

How would you describe your path?

The Elven path is unique in many ways to each individual since it is about the discovery and development of each person's individual nature. That is why we created the word *s'elf* to indicate the link between being an elf and one's true self.

The Silver Elves, Zardoa and Silver Flame

We believe in The Magic, which we define as the Infinite Potential that is the source of all things. And while most people look to escape the phenomenal world and return to the world of spirit, we elves see ours'elves as here to instil the phenomenal/material world with spirit, to master it and to create Elfin-Faerie Paradise on earth and among the stars.

So what is the elven way? It is the path that each elf chooses for hir (his or her) own s'elf. There are no rules, no requirements, other than be true to one's own s'elf. If one is true to one's s'elf, then the elf cannot go wrong. And we believe all true elves will do all in their power to help one discover that way and pursue it.

How did you first become aware of your elven natures?

Zardoa, like many elves and faerie folk, or Otherkin, as we are often called, which we like to call the elfae, became aware that he was different from the normal folk around him at a very early age. However, it took some time for him to understand what exactly that difference meant and what/who he really was/is. He was a child, of course, and a boy, and he had gotten so far as being a "young man" when he realized that, try though he may, and he did for a while, he would/could never be, nor become, a "real man." This posited the question in his mind: if he wasn't a "real man," what was he? He had to be a real *something*. Alas, it took years of searching, initiation into three different forms of meditation, and the exploration of various spiritual paths before he discovered what exactly that was.

In early 1975, he came upon two letters posted outside of an occult bookshop in Carbondale, Illinois. The letters were by the Elf Queen's Daughters and bore an address to which he replied. They responded shortly thereafter, and after a few months of back and forth correspondence, they arranged for him to come visit with them at their home in Aurora, Illinois. Four elves lived there at the time, and in the course of the weekend he spent with them, without any urging on their part, he came to realize he was/is an elf.

This was not a simple realization, however, but a full-fledged awakening of deep psychological impact that made him realize that not only was he an elf and that he had finally found his people, but that that information had been hidden within him his whole life waiting for that moment, those events, to come and trigger this awareness. Due to this profound awakening, he has dedicated his life to awakening other elves and elfae and to the continuation and development of the elven culture.

Silver Flame's awakening came a few years after Zardoa's. She did not have a sense of not fitting into society as he did, however; her sense of integrity and her devotion to human beings and their welfare over the needs of institutions and their expediencies led her into conflict with the academic institutions where she was employed over and over again.

In 1978, she came to think that an academic career was not the right thing for her, and she decided to go on a vision quest, holding in her mind the vision of a Native American shaman à la Carlos Castaneda's Don Juan, whom she expected she would meet. Instead, she came upon an elfin shaman named Zardoa. She realized then that she was an elf, and it gave her a realization of why she and her sister had made faerie houses when they were children.

Now, some thirty-five years after Zardoa's awakening in a world in which almost no one recognized their elfin being, there are elves, faeries, and others all over the globe. That we have had some small part in this awakening through our books and other writings, and through the giving of elf names (we have given over 5,000 elf names to elves all over the world), is greatly pleasing to us, and we feel privileged and delighted to be participating in this great dharma, the awakening of the elven people, and thus the re-emergence of Faery.

Why is connection to the elves and the world of Faery
so important in our modern world?

Asking why the connection to elves and the world of Faery is so important in the modern world is like asking why love, beauty, creativity, honor, fairness, joy, happiness, friendship, play, vision, hope, delight, and wonder are important to the world. And the answer is that these things, these values, these virtues are at the heart of what it means to be elfin. They are also the ultimate goals of humanity, what we live for, and, perhaps more importantly in this time, the means by which we may truly move beyond the mysterious puzzle, the malady of spirit that plagues humanity and threatens to destroy it.

There is not a call to Faery that goes unheeded, there is not a person who steps toward it that it withdraws from. It is equally true that while Elfin/Faery exists all around us in potential, it also exists within us, and curiously it is usually only by finding it within us that we can see it about us. Or to put it another way, if we can't see it within us, we will only see it apart from and without us.

This is where elfin magic comes in, for magic is a combination of action, will, and intention, and when we will to be elves and live our lives as elves with intention, we become, by magic, ever more elfin—that is to say, ever more in touch with our elfin natures, our true s'elves, and in this way increasingly in tune to the power that is Elfin/ Faery.

So why is our connection to the modern world so important? Because we represent an opportunity for a better, more loving, fulfilling, and exciting life for all who wish to embrace it. And why is the modern world so important to the elves? Because this is where we are now. This is where our dharma and duty lives at the moment, where evolution and destiny have brought us, and we intend to do our best, as we ever do, to make the most of it.

We have been told numerous times, and often by quite educated folk, without the slightest shred of scientific evidence, that there will always be war because it is part of human nature to go to war. This is the most amazing nonsense, and while we do not wish to take away anyone's right to live in a world of constant conflict and turmoil, they will not find the elven there. We are here to create Elfin-Faery Paradise on earth, and those who are determined to live in a world of war will only ever see us in their dreams in those brief and fleeting moments when they dare to believe there can be a better world.

. . . .

For more information, visit silverelves.angelfire.com.

Tië Eldaliéva, the Elven Spiritual Path

Tië eldaliéva, or the Elven Spiritual Path, is a path based entirely on the works of Tolkien, most specifically his lesser-known work *The Silmarillion*, as a valid mythology, or set of spiritual teachings accessed through story. This is a fine example of an individual path that has been created as the result of personal resonance derived from existing material that has gone on to inspire others. To quote from the website: "This is not a role-playing game (RPG) or a work of fiction, but rather an actual spiritual path for anyone who wishes to travel it, and experience it, on a very practical level."

Tië eldaliéva works specifically with the beings known as the elves, or quendi, who are of celestial origin, and though they acknowledge the close relationship with Faery beings that might be considered more akin to nature spirits or elementals, it is not the focus of their path. There are clear parallels with the noble Faery races such as the sidhe or the Nordic alfar, whose origins may also be considered to be of the stars. I spoke to the founder of this path, Lisa Allen, also known within her tradition as Calantirniel, about her inspiration and beliefs.

When did you first realise that there was more to Tolkien's work than simply fantasy?

It was entirely unexpected, that is for sure! It was in April of 2005 when I finally got around to reading *The Silmarillion* on my husband's suggestion. The original idea of reading the elven origin stories was to educate me particularly about the elven archetype shown in Tolkien's more popular stories. However, when I actually read the words, I could actually feel something happening to me, and at first it was sort of scary. It is hard to explain, but it would be likened to my blood, my DNA, just opening up and "singing" —and an overwhelming message was relayed to me that this was not imagination, this was *real*! I attempted to rationalize this feeling away and tried to tell myself (like anyone else would) that this wasn't happening and that these were just made-up stories, but this feeling got stronger and more insistent the more I tried to refute it, and I finally arrived at the conclusion that not only were these stories real, but that this was the spiritual direction I was supposed to explore!

I was not prepared for this at first and wondered if others felt this way when they read these materials too. Luckily, after searching online for a couple weeks or so, I found people who were not embarrassed to have arrived at the same conclusion as me! That was the humble beginnings of tië eldaliéva, the Elven Spiritual Path. Frankly, we thought others must have done this before. While we had found evidence that some parts of Tolkien's works were integrated into other existing Pagan-themed traditions during the 1970s at the earliest, we failed at finding any tradition based wholly on what Tolkien termed "the Legendarium," or the whole of the Middle-Earth stories.

Why is the message of his books relevant today?

I was also curious about this question—not just "why me?" but "why now?" In digging deeper with the Legendarium writings, it is apparent that the age cycles that Tolkien presented could be overlayed or correlated with those that have different origins, and we are not the first to discover this. Virtually everyone now knows the significance of 2012 being a huge turning point for the planet, shown not only by world mythologies

Julia Jeffrey,
"Dawntreader"

(especially the Mayan one, which narrowed the dates down the most) but also by science. Within the approximate 26,000-year cycle that our solar system revolves around Alcyon, the Central Sun, the year 2012 could be likened to a solstice point. So for 13,000 years the energies flowed one way, and this is the turning point for them to flow the other way. While the prophecies for this time are understandably rather dramatic, I remain hopeful and have made a conscious decision to live with my heart rather than my head—and that is what everyone can do to welcome this time in the best way possible. For those that the Elven Path resonates, it is one method to live through your heart!

What is it about Tolkien's elves that resonates with you?

I have looked into what is termed "otherkin," and while I can appreciate the philosophy, I do not feel this is an identity—only a path to travel. While I love the fact that some or even all humans could possibly have elven DNA, science cannot demonstrate this today. Instead, the way I (and a handful of others) resonate with elvenness is in wanting to learn the inherent wisdom and foresightedness, as well as embrace their balanced expression of beauty and harmony with nature, magick, and technology. While we are mortal humans, making it hard to be as wise as immortal elves, nonetheless we can still strive for that!

How aware do you think Tolkien was of what he was writing?

Actually, this was shown to me by Tolkien himself. Listening online to the Tolkien Professor, there is an introductory lecture wherein Tolkien had begun writing these stories much earlier than their publishing dates—I believe 1917 is the earliest of these writings we know of, and these were while he was in a war in a trench! He also had pictures of how he traversed to what he called "Fearie," which is what can be likened to Faery. When prompted by his Inkling colleagues about questions in the stories, Tolkien did not respond with "Oh, I need to rework that." He actually said, "Oh, I need to go *find out*"…

. . . .

For more information, visit www.ElvenSpirituality.com.

Feri Tradition and T. Thorn Coyle

"God is self and self is God and God is a person like myself."
Victor and Cora Anderson, founders of the Feri Tradition

· · · · · · ·

The Feri tradition (spelt in this unusual way to prevent confusion with other groups and traditions), a modern tradition inspired by traditional Witchcraft, was founded in California in the 1950s by Victor and Cora Anderson. They worship a celestial Goddess (whom they refer to as "God herself") and her consorts, divine twins of light and dark who contain both male and female within them.

There are many parallels to be found with their beliefs and the Jewish mystical system of Qabalah, including the power of polarity and the Triple Soul—that is, that the human soul comprises three parts: the *nephesh*, which is the basic energy of life that stays with the body after death; the *ruach*, which is the spirit; and the *neshamah*, which is the higher self and connected to the world soul. In Feri tradition they refer to these three parts of the soul as *unuhipili*, *ke uhane mulama*, and *aumakua*, showing a great influence of Hawaiian *Huna*, a Hawaiian shamanic tradition.

Feri also contains elements from many other magickal traditions of the world, including Voudou and Italian Witchcraft, and they greatly revere the peacock angel Melek-Taus, leading to mistaken and inaccurate associations with Satanism. It would be more accurate to connect this with the association we discussed earlier with Faery, the world soul and "fallen" angels, Melek-Taus being strongly linked with Lucifer.

The Feri tradition seeks to liberate and empower the individual to embody their full potential as divine human beings. One of the most inspiring modern teachers to emerge from this tradition is the popular and internationally respected T. Thorn Coyle. The author of *Kissing the Limitless* and *Evolutionary Witchcraft*, she hosts the *Elemental Castings* podcast series; writes a popular weblog, *Know Thyself*; and has produced several CDs of sacred music. Thorn's spiritual direction, soul reading, and body/spirit coaching practices help people worldwide. Pagan, mystic, and activist, she is founder and head of Solar Cross Temple and Morningstar Mystery School and lives by the San Francisco Bay. Though she now teaches her own magickal tradition, she shared some insights into the Feri tradition, what she learned from it, and the directions in which life and work are taking her now.

Shay Skepevski,
"Peacock Vision"

What do you feel you've learned from your long involvement with the Feri tradition?

I have learned that diligent practice is necessary to maintain one's sense of growth and equilibrium when the power and energy we are capable of accessing begins to move through our lives. People who don't keep up with foundational practice are often bowled over by the power that opening to clear streams of life force and magick open up. I also gained a deeper appreciation for the presence of the realms seen and unseen, and how all participate in the divine emanation through space and time.

How did it help you to develop your own methods that
you now teach? What do your teachings offer?

Anderson Feri tradition and the teachings of Victor and Cora have had a huge impact on my life. The concept that our soul has facets that need to be explored and brought into alignment is a core teaching that I use each day. The reclaiming of the energies of sex, pride, self, power, and passion has also had a profound impact.

We have the power and ability to live with strength, effectiveness, and integrity in full alignment with all parts of our soul. The fact that there exist practices to help us deepen and balance our connection to this power is even bigger.

This weaves through my work, coupled with steady self-observation, meditation, and the idea that God Herself is present in all things, and we therefore have a responsibility to co-create the universe with the gods, nature, and the totality of divine flow. We can come into full possession of our own divine selves, living in harmony with all the realms, and taking our rightful place in the unfolding of the cosmos.

You seem to put a good deal of emphasis on empowerment and
self-awareness. How does that expand into awareness of Faery?

I once asked Victor Anderson what the Fey wanted from me, and he replied: "For you to become more yourself. For you to become more human." That hit me strongly! For me to live in greater harmony with all the realms means I have to live in greater harmony within myself! That, to me, is what the tools and practices of magick are for: to become fully ourselves so we can actually be of help to other beings.

Our work is not about running off into other realms but about bringing ourselves and our own realms into the greatest health and balance possible so that we can better share space with all the realms.

T. Thorn Coyle

How would you describe your relationship with Faery?

My relationship is that of the poet to the muse, the warrior to the fire of courage, and the human soul to nature. Faery connects me to the light in the land and the possibility of beauty. It also is helpful to me in that it affords an opportunity for my sceptical brain to hold space with my imagination and with energetic and emotional experiences. It is good to doubt the reality of the unseen realms and simultaneously stretch my mind to include rationally inexplicable happenings. Making space for dissonance keeps us strong and flexible. I have experiences of Faery and can also hold that these perceptions feel irrational. I'm okay with that.

Why is working with the seven directions important?

The seven sacred directions help to orient us in space and time. We have a center at our core and a circumference that extends 360 degrees around us. If I can maintain awareness of the horizon all around me, as well as above and below, I can remain centered in my life and my work, and remain in relationship with everything I interact with. The seven directions remind me that my whole life is about this relationship. I don't just focus on what is in front of me but interact with all spaces around me, including what is just beyond the edge of my perception. Working with the seven sacred directions also serves as a link to magick workers of old, who studied the seven visible planets or intoned the seven vowels or walked through the seven gates or called upon the seven angels. It connects us to our magickal legacy and opens us to what is yet to come. The seven directions also help me remember that there is more to the world than my eyes and ears perceive. There is possibility all around me in every moment.

What change would you like to bring into the world?

I would like for connection to become deeply important. I would like for each human to practice internal alignment so that our relationship to the world can come into greater alignment, so that our relationship with all the worlds can come into greater alignment. We can be strong, autonomous, compassionate, and free, living in right relationship, bringing our systems of imbalance toward integration. I would like for more and more people to want this change and actively work toward its fulfilment. I'll keep starting with myself.

· ·

For further information, visit www.thorncoyle.com.

The Resurgence of Faery Inspiration

*"It is Credibly Asserted, that in ancient times that many
of those aforesaid Gnomes, Fairies Elves & other terrestrial
wandering spirits, have been seen & heard amongst Men,
but now it is said & believed that they are not so frequent."*

The seventeenth-century Sloane MS 3825

· · · · · · ·

It seems that every generation for the last several hundred years has commented on the dwindling relationship between humans and faeries, and yet most of the traditions, groups, and paths we have looked at in this chapter were either born or have grown immensely in popularity over the last half century! While all are expressed in diverse ways, what all these paths have in common is the theme of uncovering and embracing our true selves in order to be more fully in the world. When we can truly know and be ourselves, we can find what it is we are here to do. We can then use these gifts to build a bridge to the realm of Faery, just as the following inspirational artists, musicians, writers, entertainers, and craftspeople are doing through their work. May their words inspire you to find your soul's true expression and bring potential to full bloom!

The Artists

There are many incredible artists working within the Faery community today, each with their own distinctive style and approach, yet all drawing their inspiration from the same source: the realm of Faery. I was lucky enough to be able to interview a few of the most influential and inspirational figures in the world of Faery art today, and here I share with you a glimpse into the lives of the people behind the beautiful art.

Brian and Wendy Froud

Brian and Wendy Froud are loved and respected around the world, bringing joy and inspiration to many through their many years of sharing their visions of Faery with the world. Brian is a fine artist and illustrator perhaps best known for his work as a conceptual artist in the 1980s hit movies *Labyrinth* and *The Dark Crystal*, as well as many beautiful published works, including *Faeries* (with Alan Lee), *Good Fairies/Bad Faeries*, *The Faeries Oracle* (with Jessica Macbeth), and most recently *How To See Fairies* (with John Matthews).

Wendy is a doll artist, sculptor, and puppet-maker extraordinaire, with many published works to her name, including *The Winter Child* and *The Faeries of Spring Cottage*, as well as a recent collaboration with Brian on the *Heart of Faery Oracle*. Not only has Wendy worked alongside Brian on *Labyrinth* and *The Dark Crystal*, but she was one of the original team of sculptors who created Yoda for *The Empire Strikes Back*! I visited Brian and Wendy in their beautiful hobbitlike home in rural Devon, UK, to gain some insight into their creative process and relationship with Faery.

I'm not going to bother asking if you believe in faeries, because we know you do...

B: People assume I'm just illustrating something, and I say no, I'm *expressing* something. There's a big difference. Now we've just got this book out with John Matthews called *How To See Faeries*, there's no way around it. Right now people are saying, "Ah, these people really do believe in faeries and are telling us about it," and that, I think, has been a breakthrough in getting people to understand we do believe.

How did your awareness of the Faery realm first enter your life?

W: For me, it came really from my mother and my mother's family. She's always believed, and she just taught me to believe from an early age. It was just the most natural thing, and it wasn't a cute little game we played or anything, it was just that they were there, and we could leave things for them, and we could feel them. We couldn't see them particularly, but we could always feel them, so I just grew up thinking it was the most natural thing in the world.

B: I don't know, because in Faery time it doesn't make any sense whatsoever. However, there were a couple of events that were reminders. One was when I was at art school and I was about to give up painting, because I felt that was not the right thing and not expressive of what I wanted to do, and I was going to do graphic design. As I was waiting in the college library for my interview I came across a book by Arthur Rackham, and in it were these wonderful drawings of trees with faces in, and that was the revelation. I thought, "That's how I felt as a child." I was always exploring woods, climbing trees, crawling underneath bushes, and there was something about the faces that informed you there was spirit in nature, and that got me into exploring Faery tales and more and more exploring the reality behind Faery tales and faeries themselves.

The next thing was when I moved to Dartmoor and I experienced nature—rocks and trees and roots and earth—and I realised that I didn't want to be a normal landscape painter, I wanted to paint the landscape that was the inner landscape. I wanted to know what it looked like on the inside, and once I felt that, then I started to paint trolls and faeries.

I discovered faeries really by making it up, by trying to imagine what it was…but it was always about feeling. So I brought all my skills as an artist to bear on trying to get the form and shape of what I was painting to feel like something that was elusive and invisible. Then I did various pictures, paintings, bits of books, and then the book, the *Faeries* book. Alan Lee and myself just tumbled into it, just went for it. We did research, we were both enthusiastic about English, Irish, and Scottish folklore, and we just worked from the descriptions that people had given over the years and drew it.

I think because we did it with passion and insight, we were getting it right, and people really responded to it. But it was only really years later when I embarked upon another book, called *Good Faeries/Bad Faeries*, which was more about my inner world-view of faeries, more about how I was feeling about them, and it was more of a spiritual thing, and again I did it really through intuition. It's really only when that was finished and I was on tour with the book and signing the book, I started to spontaneously experience faeries on the streets of America!

W: That's the book you have to write, that's the book I want you to write someday! It is amazing, the story.

B: It is a rare thing for me to have those spontaneous Faery experiences, but they are real.

So really you are translating a feeling into a visual interpretation, which creates that same feeling in the viewer, creating a bridge in that way?

W: Very much so, they are a bridge to the otherworld, or a doorway, a gateway. Very often with our work, people will look at it and they will have a very emotional response when they experience it. It's something about "coming home." It's something about going to a place that they forgot they knew so well. That's wonderful.

Wendy Froud, "Autumn"

How well do think you've portrayed you feelings or your vision
of the otherworld—how close do you think you've got?

W: I don't think it's anything like what they really are, only how they appear. Sometimes I think they do look like that, but usually they are energy. It's impossible, I think, especially in three dimensions, it's impossible to capture it because so much of it is the energy, and you can't really sculpt that.

B: Well, I think I've got nowhere near! After all these years I haven't got anywhere near, but I keep trying. People want to believe what I'm showing them is real, and they go, "Oh, that's how they look, isn't it?" and I say, "Well, actually, no. It's how they *feel*." You've got to bring people to some place where they can understand and feel it, and also that is a genuine opening, a genuine gateway to the reality—not only to the wider reality but to that specific or particular personality.

A genuine experience of Faery seems to be clear whilst it's happening, but afterwards it's impossible to express. It seems vague because so many different aspects come to bear in that experience, it isn't just a visual thing, it's an "other" thing—an other thing of otherness! The problem is when you try to express any of this stuff, everything fails. Words fail, pictures fail, everything is failing in one of the most astonishing and beautiful events. So to do what I do is trying to do the impossible, but I believe in it passionately.

Often the paintings are either doorways or, in the more complex ones, maps. They're maps into Faeryland that you explore and you follow shapes. Shapes are very important in what I do because it's the abstractions. I put geometry in so when you look at one of the pictures it isn't just surface, it's something that happens underneath that propels you not just deep into Faeryland but out into the cosmos. What I try to do is something mystical.

Faery art in particular needs to be expressive of—well, of Faery! People have a preconceived idea of what they should be, and they don't like anything that challenges that idea. But the idea is incredibly recent, faeries have been with us forever and been part of our spiritual life as well as part of our cultural life.

I've been thinking of this a lot—obviously with my own work, thinking about the journey of our relationship with Faery—and it seems to me that it all changed around the Industrial Revolution. There's this idea of trying to tame nature, and that's perhaps when we started trying to tame faeries too...

B: I haven't got an answer to that, that really fascinates me. It does seem to me that the Industrial Revolution is a bit of a watershed. There is lots of folklore evidence of faeries and Faery creatures that are in the country in that period, but not any evidence of them being in the cotton mills, for instance, and there should be. Did people, as they moved from the country, bring spirits with them or not? They don't seem to, or it's been hidden. They don't seem to show up in the industrial landscape.

W: Too much iron...

You've seen them on the streets of America—in an urban environment?
W: Very much so!

B: Always. One of the ones that was odd, I can't remember exactly where it was but it was on the East Coast. I was walking down the street and I felt there were leprechauns around. I thought, "That's really stupid, why would there be leprechauns on the edge of America?" Then I saw a plaque on a pole standing there in this weird long, open space, and it said, "On this site were the fever sheds." It's when the Irish immigrants were coming in on boats, and they had yellow fever. They were put in the sheds to die, basically, to isolate them. They brought the leprechauns with them!

That's interesting, isn't it, because we know that faeries are connected to the land but clearly they are also connected to us ancestrally...

B: It does seem that people bring their faeries with them, because I had another experience around San Francisco which was again a leprechaun, but he was on the edge of a field and a wood and my conversations with him were always on the edge of the day, always the morning, sitting there with a cup of coffee and thinking about things. The actual physical place was a hundred yards away from where I was sitting, but there was a conversation that would happen with a leprechaun. It was distinctly a leprechaun, with all the accoutrements—the tricorn hat became quite important in his communications with me. It was just fascinating. But it was a leprechaun! Why? But you can't question

Wendy Froud, "Bad Faery"

this stuff—you can try, but you just have to trust it. If you don't get it, it's you being stupid because there'll be a moment where there'll be some revelation and you'll think, "Yes, of course! That's what it was trying to say!"

Is it that the spirits travel with people, do you think, or is it that the spirits
of that place choose familiar forms from our own subconscious, or based
on the people they've had contact with, to communicate with us?

W: It could be either one…probably both…

B: Yes, absolutely both. The pure energy is unintelligible; you need form, you need some intelligible form.

W: That's why we can portray things.

B: So either you can provide the form as the human aspect, or they provide the form. Sometimes the form is truly expressive of its nature, and sometimes its form is not an expression of its nature, it's just a way of allowing you into the space so that you can understand its inner nature.

Like a mask?
B: Yes.

Do you have practices that maintain your connection with Faery?
W: We do leave offerings in the garden, yes. But I think that because of where we live, because that energy is just a constant here with us, we don't have to be conscious of it all the time. We really do just live with it, and it's a part of where we live. I think that if we moved, or if we were in another place for long enough, we'd have to be more aware of it and very consciously try to communicate. Whereas here, we don't really…we share the space with them.

B: Generally everything we do is about Faery…it's just continuous, so we don't have to do things deliberately.

W: Although it's interesting because when we do go out into the circle and do ritual, the energy is just amazing. We had a blessing ceremony that John and Caitlín

(Matthews) did as part of a wedding, and since then the energy has been so much stronger and more focused.

B: They did a Faery blessing for the wedding, and I think that lots of people who were invited didn't know what to expect, and everybody was amazed.

W: And I think a lot of people felt that they were restating their own vow at the same time, so it was like a collective blessing for everyone. It was wonderful.

B: Also, people tend to think faeries are "airy fairy," and what was happening was a reconnection to the land itself—people felt they were connected to their own landscape. People just love that, they were moved by it.

Do you have particular beings that you work with or is it a variety of beings that come forward at different times?

W: For me they just come forward when they need to; I don't have one that's there to help all the time. There's so many! They all want a turn, they want to come forward and push their way to the front.

B: I had one that came back with me, a few years ago, from America. It came and stayed a long time in the house. I promised to take it back if it ever wanted to go back, and it wanted to go back, so I took it back to where it had come from. So that had been very helpful. I'm not a person who constantly dwells on it or checks in. When I do check in occasionally, it's always astonishing when these beings are there and imparting something, some help. So now I have another one! There always seems to be one special one, for a while anyway.

How do you find that you influence and support each other?

W: I think we've worked together in many ways since we've been together, which is over thirty years now—such a long time! But we've only just recently begun to collaborate on projects together to this extent. To write about Brian's work I find fascinating because I hadn't really done that before; I did it for the oracle deck and really enjoyed it. We have to be aware of each other's egos when we're working together, really, because we both have a tendency to be able to point out exactly what's wrong with the other person's work but if you say it in the wrong way we would just storm off into our studios and then later on go, "Oh, you were right, you were right!"

How would you like to develop your work in the future? What would you like to achieve?

W: It would be nice to do film again, something new that goes even further than we went before…

Can it have Bowie in tight trousers again?

W: Yeah, maybe…he's older now. Maybe Johnny Depp?

B: It's problematic trying to think of doing something in three dimensions and in movement. I'm in despair when I see how films are made now and how you do it. But it still, one hopes, can be done. I was just in London at the Little Angel Puppet Theatre, and they showed *Labyrinth*. They said they could have sold the tickets time after time because they only did one showing. It's just how people responded to it. To try and figure out what it is about *Labyrinth* and *Dark Crystal*, it's the thing that you don't see. You're looking at a movie, but you're also feeling something else. It's that other magic that went on that's beneath the surface and about how you get that onscreen. It came from a different direction, whereas many people who make movies now, it's about money and market research and all this stuff but not allowing the mystery to shine through. It would be wonderful to be able to attempt to do something that was slightly out of your grasp when you were making it, and you didn't quite understand it. Those films have had longevity because they were not of their time, they were of another time that's fluid and therefore continues to be timeless. It's intriguing to think, is it possible to do something like that again? I don't know…

I just want whatever I do to have meaning, to have resonance. Having said that, what we find is, whatever we do, it seems to go into a book. I believe passionately in books as a way of communicating ideas to people, but they want to be out doing different things. They want to be part of people's lives. Any way of allowing that to happen, I'm all for it!

For more information, visit www.worldoffroud.com.

Kelly Martinez and Marc Potts

Marc Potts and Kelly Martinez

Marc Potts is a visionary artist based in the UK, whose powerful work is informed by his exceptional knowledge of folklore and connection to the spirits of the land. His work has appeared on numerous book covers and Pagan publications, and he is currently working towards several books of his own. Kelly Martinez, Marc's partner, is an exceptionally skilled jeweller and master pattern maker, specialising in ancient methods that are little known in the modern world. I interviewed this fascinating and talented couple about their creative work and experiences of Faery.

Marc Potts, "Old Ginny"

What does Faery mean to you?

K: It's something that's always been with me. I don't know where it comes from, there's no one else in my family that feels this way. I was always the odd kid at school! I have always, from being tiny, known that there was something other than human or animal—spirit that is nature based. I've always felt very close to that. Especially when I'm out on my native moors, the West Yorkshire moors, like Saddleworth Moor. It's like electricity going through me, and I know it's not just coming from the land, but there are other things there. Elementals, whatever you want to call them, but there is something else there. It's something very spiritual. It's part of me.

M: To me, very much the same sort of thing. It's a nature-based spirituality. I've always had an affinity with not just nature, but I was fascinated by the whole landscape, the spirit of the landscape. I started on this path a long time ago…late seventies, early eighties. I never called faeries "faeries," usually nature spirits or elementals. Elementals is a word I use a lot.

It was a form of invented Paganism, I didn't follow any particular path within Paganism and still don't, but there's elements of lots of different paths within Paganism that have elementals and Faery lore. My ritual work would centre around elementals, not just earth, air, fire, water, and all that business, but elementals of rocks or a tree—especially trees. Everything has a spirit, and there's almost hierarchies of spirits. There's what I would call a "landscape Pan," which would be above certain other things, for example. The art that I do, that's my way of manifesting…I had to paint it. Also, I'm an avid reader of folklore; I read anything and everything. It's not necessarily Pagan, but it ties in. You can recognise the old gods sometimes, they're everywhere. It's not just little faeries in dresses—they rarely are.

What do you see as being the purpose of your creations? Why do you do what you do?

M: This is going to sound flaky, but I kind of made a deal after a ritual I did one day. I was in Wales…again, this was the early eighties, we decided in this ritual we were all going to take on different roles, and I was the Horned God. After that I did these four paintings…I used to be a natural history artist, but these were the first "Pagan" type paintings I'd done. They were tree spirits. I gave those four paintings to my friend, and then there was a subsequent ritual, which was all about what I was going to do from then on. It was a deal I made…it's a one-sided deal, but it's certainly satisfying in a driven sort of way.

I used to do a lot of "sitting out"…going out into the wilderness, staying out all night. You do get some fantastic stuff from that. I used to do a lot of trance work. I used to do this thing with tree spirits, for instance—I would befriend a particular tree, and over a period of weeks I would keep returning to that tree and meditating or visualising or trance or whatever happened, and I would do paintings from that. Sometimes a face would just loom out of the darkness at me. There was a particular holly tree…people wouldn't be able to tell it was a holly spirit, but I knew.

K: Sometimes I wish I was a painter! I was supposed to go into some kind of television production, but having a father who was a goldsmith—a Spanish goldsmith, too, so different techniques than were being taught in the UK—I decided to rebel against what was expected and asked to do a formal apprenticeship at a time when the skills were being lost from the UK. So that's how I ended up doing my job, never knowing if I'd take to it or not.

My dad threw me in at the deep end and gave me a piece of antique jewellery to copy. Now, my work is in wax, I'm a master pattern maker and use the lost wax-carving process. It's one of the oldest techniques of making jewellery, and I took to it straightaway. My dad couldn't believe that I had managed to copy this piece of jewellery, as I wasn't interested before then. I absolutely loved it, and he couldn't believe there was this latent talent!

As well as this apprenticeship, which took between five and eight years, he said, "Develop your own style." I loved the work of Lalique; it was the closest thing I'd found that touched on how I felt about nature spirits. He and his workers had really tapped into something, at that point, with art nouveau. Also, Mucha designed the most amazing jewellery…there was this time in history when nature was so revered, and I really got that. I also started to get really interested in folklore.

I'm not brilliant at drawing or painting, I just can't visualise in two dimensions, and this sculptural technique meant that I could sculpt my visions into jewellery. And these would end up facilitating other people's paths, other people's spiritual growth, as they would always ask questions about the symbols in the work. And at the end of the day, I'm learning all the time.

Marc Potts,
"Hedgerider"

"Myth of the Magpie" (TOP LEFT) and "Let Me
Sing You a Tale of True Love" by Kelly Martinez

How close do you think you've got in your work to your experiences of Faery?

M: The tree spirits—it's all very personal, but to me that was spot-on. Whether or not that would be spot-on for the next man or woman, I don't know or care, for that matter. I wasn't doing it for anybody apart from them—and me.

K: The elements are a huge part of what I do. When you look at the history of metal smithing, we could make objects that would destroy or create that were objects of power. And I am talking as a jewellery smith, not a blacksmith. Look at an object of power, the magic that it has in it. We take a metal that is from the earth, we use fire to melt it, air to give strength to the fire, then we quench it afterwards with water. You can lose yourself in that process, there's a lot of magic in those items. You are working directly with the elements, you're working with the gods, goddesses, and the elementals.

. . . .

For more information, visit www.marcpotts.com and www.kellymartinez.co.uk.

Linda Ravenscroft

Linda Ravenscroft is a much-beloved member of the Faery community, with her exceptionally finely detailed Faery art and distinctive art nouveau style. Her published works include *The Mystic Faery Tarot* (with Barbara Moore) and *How to Draw and Paint Fairies*, and her art may also be found worldwide on greetings cards and prints. She kindly spared some time at the Three Wishes Faery Fest in Cornwall to answer some questions about her work.

When did you start drawing faeries and why?

I never actually started to draw faeries ever. It wasn't my intention! I've always just drawn stuff for me. When I was little I was bullied at school, so I used to go home and draw. You don't tell people that you're being picked on, but I used to go home and just go to my special place. I suppose it was like a fairyland, but it was where I was safe and beautiful, a princess with a handsome prince, you name it! It was fantasy, it was fabulous…a place for me.

I've always loved painting fantasy goddesses and always loved nature, so that started to come into my work. You see trees as living things, and then you start adding faces and bodies to them, and before I knew it I'd done a dryad and I didn't even know it! The faeries found me, I didn't find them, and I didn't go out to paint them—they've always been there, and they have to come out at the right time.

I've never even seen a real faerie, but I don't need to because they just automatically come out. People can interpret them anyway they like, but what really excites me is that people will pick out the image they really need in their lives. A lot of my paintings are personal, about things that are happening to me and around me. The funny thing is people pick up on it as well, and it's so magical when someone knows what a piece is about before you've even told them. They're not just pretty faeries, it's a lot deeper and hopefully more inspirational. It's something I want to share desperately with people. And it's a good message.

I don't do dark, I really don't. I've never been in a really black space, actually, when I've wanted to paint something dark. What I truly want is to make people feel better. There's too much darkness in the world as it is, and we need to be lifted more. Things are getting really low at the moment, and we need to balance it. To give someone a hopeful

Linda Ravenscroft in her studio

Linda Ravenscroft,
"Mistress Winter and Jack Frost"

image—it must make them feel better to know there are beautiful things out there and there are things and people that care.

How important do you feel the artist's role is within the Faery community?

Well, I think it really is important. People have their own ideas about faeries, perhaps what they are brought up with, Disney and things like that. As they get older, perhaps they still adore the idea of Tinker Bell, but when they can see it from a more practical perspective as well, this is a good thing. It's about looking after our beautiful world that we're all living in, looking after each other. So it's great for us to show them things that they might not have the ability to imagine themselves or see for themselves. They can see it in our artwork.

I've had people create outfits based on my faeries. I had a phoenix turn up at one of the lovely events, she made the whole outfit of the phoenix. I thought, she's been inspired to create this from my creativity! Things like this are just irreplaceable. So, yes, the artists have to be here. Not just myself as a visual artist from the point of view of being two dimensional, there's the three-dimensional crafts and things as well. You can't buy things like this on the street. I feel very passionate about it!

Where do you draw inspiration from?

It's all to do with what's going on in the world, I think. It's the way I see things. The last thing I want to do is to start saying to people, "You should do this, you should do that"—you don't want to start preaching to people. I can emit my personal feelings into my artwork very personally, very quietly, and then I can show people, and they usually get the message without me needing to say a word.

People as well—people that you meet at festivals. Also, I love getting together with other artists and chatting! I'd love to do an exhibition on a subject, with every artist invited to produce one piece, and I'd love the public to go round and try to guess which artist produced which piece! Everything is so individual, that's why there's no competition between us, there's no animosity or anything like that, because we know that even if we produce the same idea, it will be so different.

What do you like about the Faery festivals?

Before we had the festivals we had no way to show our art. We were fortunate enough to have the Internet, but you want to share it with people. We're never taken seriously in the art world, so finding a gallery in London or somewhere like that that's likely to take your work is really hard, and it's not treated as a serious form of art. But when you can have a festival like this, it's encouraging for us to know that there are people out there who really do need and want this art. I think that is important—we've just got to share it with people. The more people we can introduce to it, I think the better the whole world's going to feel, don't you?

. . . .

For more information, visit www.lindaravenscroft.com.

Linda Ravenscroft,
"The Queen of Leaves"

The Musicians

Where would all the Faery balls and festivals around the world be without the musicians and bands to dance our hooves off to? There are many wonderful bands and musicians in the Faery community, playing everything from gentle classical harp to heavy rock!

The Dolmen

The Dolmen are a familiar and welcome sight at most Pagan and Faery events throughout the UK and Europe, and they are also starting to become known in the US. They are famed for their driving rhythms and wicked piratical flair, playing an irresistible blend of folk and Celtic themes and original material with a hard-rock edge. The Dolmen consist of Tony "Taloch" Jameson on lead vocals and guitar (he's also the songwriter); Keri Pinney on flute, whistle, and vocals; Kayleigh Marchant on bass guitar and vocals; Josh Elliot on guitar, mandolin, and vocals (he's also a songwriter); and Chris Jones on drums. I caught the band after an exhausting night playing at the Three Wishes Faery Fest in Cornwall to find out what makes them tick. Though all the band were present, Taloch did most of the talking.

How did you get started?

The original concept of the Dolmen was started a couple of decades ago, but it's only in its current strength in the present lineup that we have now, because for the first time the whole band is gelling. The unison where everybody thinks together has brought the Dolmen back to a very organic performance onstage, which means that we don't actually rehearse our songs. They happen live. Because the band has gelled in that way, we're able to work it out as we go. That's what the Dolmen is about.

Do you all share similar spiritual beliefs?

We're very, very spiritually involved and always have been. We actually put on two of our own spiritual festivals per year—the Beltane Spirit of Rebirth and the Tribal Dreams Gathering. It's a nice time at the moment, actually, especially in the UK, because you have this wonderful energy of Faery magic and the whole Faery spirit, which is a big part of what the Dolmen is about. The girls are very much into the Faery line, whereas on the male side, we're pirates in a very spiritual way. These two things work brilliantly. Also, we're allowed access once a year as the Dolmen into Stonehenge. They allow us to have two hours where we take in many members of mixed spiritual paths within the Faery Pagan concept…free thinkers.

Do you play all over the world?

We basically go anywhere! We have an extensive tour coming up next month, which takes us into Europe. Also, next year we have lined up some tours into the States, and we have a gig in Iceland, which is going to be quite nice, lined up for next year. As far as we can, we go!

For more information, visit www.thedolmen.com.

The Dolmen

Elizabeth-Jane Baldry and her harp, Oberon

Elizabeth-Jane Baldry

Elizabeth-Jane Baldry is an extraordinary woman with many strings to her bow…or, indeed, her harp. Not only is she a talented classical harpist, but she also runs her own filmmaking company, Chagford Filmmaking Group, in which she produces, directs, writes, composes, and performs the score, and even edits the footage! Her work has taken her to events all over the world. We had a good long talk about her sources of inspiration and how she got to where she is today.

Which came first for you, was it the love of music or the love of Faery?

I loved fairies right from as soon as I was born; I spent hours looking for them when I was a little girl! But I loved harp as well, and the two were completely, in my mind, connected.

How do you feel your harp playing connects to the land of Faery?
Does it work on a personal level or does it affect others as well?

I think that the harp is particularly subtle as an instrument of Faery; the very sound of it seems to thin the veil between the worlds. It's fascinating that in cultures around the world the harp has always been associated with the otherworld. For example, the royal harpist in Mesopotamia would actually be buried with the monarch—he'd be buried alive. In the Celtic lands, the chief would be buried with a harp at their feet, because it was considered a bridge between man and the supernatural. The tension of the strings symbolized the tension that we have as humans between our spirit and earthly lives. A few years back I did a course with a musical archaeologist at Cambridge University, and he said this was true. He had dug up many harpists' graves, Anglo-Saxons, and the chieftains did have the harps at their feet, but what I learned from him was that the harpists themselves would be buried with the harp in their arms. We did reconstructions of Anglo-Saxon poetry with reconstructions of these harps with strings of plaited horse hair, a very similar sound to the gut strings of today.

Was your first experience of Faery directly connected to music?

That's an interesting question! I remember as a child just lying in the grass and that feeling of absolute oneness with nature. The hours would just pass by; I spent a lot of time outside as a child. We did have a little house at the end of the garden that my dad said the fairies lived in, that he made. It was really lovely, it had mosaics in it. I was very lucky, my parents were imaginative and supportive. We had lots of books; I could read very early, from the age of about three or four. I had this huge great big book called *The Staircase of Stories* and I loved it so much, it was all fairy stories. I used to take it to bed with me instead of teddies. It was a bit worse for wear after a few years of that! We moved house when I was five years old and sadly the book got lost in the move, and I was devastated. I told this story to my friend Ari Berk, and he found a vintage copy for me! I remembered so many of the stories even though I hadn't seen the book since I was five. It didn't seem quite so giant though!

So Faery was always with you, and the music came later as a natural extension of that?

I started piano very early, at about five or six, but piano never did it for me—I wanted to play the harp. Finally, when I was fourteen, I started learning the harp. The sound was completely magical to me, it just transported me. There's so many harps in fairy tales. Think of "Jack and the Beanstalk," the talking harp who actually reveals the crime—it's quite scary, the harp cries out! I loved that.

When you're writing music, where do you feel your inspiration is coming from?

Usually, with the concert works, I just sit in a quite space and it comes. With the film music, I look at the pictures and it comes, it does just come. It pops into my head quite easily!

Do you have a muse or ally that you consciously work with?

I would say that in my inner world I have got quite a lot of imaginative friends, if you like, that I sometimes meet in dreams or meditation.

You mentioned your film work. When did you first have the idea to produce these films?

It happened by accident because my kids were bored in the holidays. There was nothing to do, so I said, well, let's make a movie! I went over to the bookshelves—obviously it had to be a fairy film, because I love fairies and fairy tales. I pulled out the Grimm's fairy stories and it fell open on "Three Little Men in a Wood," which we adapted and made the first film, which we called *Woodwose*—made it much more wild, it's a fun little film. Enormously good fun, I just loved it! I did everything on that film: I wrote it, made the costumes, worked the camera, did the cinematography, everything.

On the strength of that I got the bursary to make a second film, and I made a lovely little charming British fairy tale called *Pottle o' Brains* about this wise woman and this fool. He goes to the wise woman to see if he can get some brains. It's a lovely, sweet little fairy tale. After that, I established the Chagford Filmmaking Group as a nonprofit community group to bring people together, and we specialized in British fairy tales because they're so rooted in the landscape we love so much.

There's no profit involved in all this work that you do on the films, so what drives you—why do you feel it's important?

It's incredibly important to me that it remains voluntary and that nobody gets paid because it brings this very beautiful energy to the films, that everyone is doing it because they love the stories. Even if they don't believe in fairies, they love nature, and the images of nature are very important to me. I really believe that these stories have a lot of wisdom in them, indigenous wisdom. They were our classroom for thousands of years, long before the digital delights of today, and fairy tales were for everyone, not just for children. This is how we learnt about ourselves and how we learnt the important lessons of life. The importance of sharing, the importance of truth, the importance of honouring nature…it's all there in these ancient stories, everything you need to know to live a good life in the deepest sense of the word. It's all there.

And courage, too. Courage to keep going, staying true even against the most terrible odds. That's what all the heroes do. And heroines! I'm very drawn to stories with resourceful heroines who manage to take charge of their own lives rather than being just being a prize for a boy who has all the fun. There's plenty of these stories about gutsy little heroines, but because they were all collected in the nineteenth century they were considered unsuitable for girls, so they're stuck to the back of the anthropology section in libraries as curiosities! I do feel that they need to come out into the open…

What is next? How are you going to develop this even further?

My end dream is to produce a body of work of films of British fairy tales that will sell on DVD and generate an income that can be used for work with young people, arts projects, and conservation, these sorts of issues. I would hope that I can get a fair few in, and they will never go out of date. There will always be children, and there will always be parents who want their children to see things that are homegrown.

· ·

For more information, visit www.fairytalefilms.co.uk.

S. J. Tucker

S. J. Tucker

S. J. Tucker is a modern-day troubador, part Faery, part pirate, part gypsy, and all talent! Her music has a distinctive folk rock style, sometimes catchy, often bardic, and is much loved around the world. She has produced a number of albums, both as a solo artist and with the band Tricky Pixie, and she often performs in both capacities at the most popular Faery events in the United States. I caught her in the midst of her usual whirlwind schedule to gain an insight into her wild and creative life.

What does Faery mean to you?

Since I perform often at events like the Faerieworlds festival in the Pacific Northwest, Faery often means community to me. When I think of Faery, I think of a field full of dancing revelers, kicking up joy and magick with their every step, rain or shine, as I sing my heart out for them. Faery is what we find when we allow the wild and feral energies within us come out to play. Faery is the side of the unknown, of magick and potential, that gives me a feeling of positive excitement. Faery is a cue to watch my step, to move in the world with a smile but with my eyes open, because I never know whom, or what, I will meet around the next shadowed corner. Faery is a word that promises a good story, regardless of whether the players in it are all silly or flat-out sinister.

There are as many sides to Faery as there are to folklore and to our own world. Not all aspects of what we call Faery are kind, but I've been lucky in my dealings and experiences thus far. When you move with awareness and respect in the world, even someplace as tricky as Faery is said to be, I find that you generally make it through without making too many blunders.

What are you trying to express in your music?

Music is the source, to me. Anytime I open my mouth to sing, I am tapping into something that exists in everyone and everything. Music gives me joy and generally makes everything better, no matter where I am or what I'm doing. When I sing, write, and play, my highest goal is to give everyone who hears me some safe ground to stand on, somewhere solid to be and to experience whatever emotions or impressions come to them. Music has the power to speak to all of us, whether it includes words in our own language, words in another language, or no words at all. I'm just another channel for it, but my hope is that the music I bring into the world brings more magick into the world when it comes and puts that magick somewhere others can find it if and when they need it.

How important are musicians within the Faery community?

Hugely important; that's certainly how the Faery community has made me feel. It's difficult not to keep coming back when one is so well-treated. The Faery festivals I work with make a conscious effort to create a temporary world and an immersive experience—for performers as well as for participants—and they bring musicians in from all over the globe to add to the magick. I'm so grateful to be part of this community, not least because I have musician friends from many other countries as a result of being adopted by and singing for Faery-friendly folk. For some, time spent at Faery festivals is the only time they can cut loose. I'm honored to provide part of the soundtrack for that. To see people spread their wings and shine—both literally and figuratively—is a great gift.

What is it like to be a pirate queen?

A girl couldn't ask for more. Since I started writing pirate songs, such as the ones I've written about Wendy taking over the pirate ship in Neverland instead of going home, I've made lifelong friends of so many beautiful, vibrant, strong women and men, who aren't afraid to put on delightfully silly costumes and wave plastic swords around. Also, there's a great deal of crossover between the fans of mine who are willing to participate in Faery events and the fans of mine who regularly dress as pirates. I would not trade them for the world.

My last concert in recent weeks as of this interview was at the aforementioned Faerieworlds festival. I performed with my band, Tricky Pixie, on the "deck" of a pirate ship stage that was making its first appearance at the festival this year. Our crowd came out in force and wore their pirate garb proudly, despite the fact that rain threatened, and they sang along with every word. You can't beat a life such as this. Real and historic pirates never had it so good.

. . . .

For more information, visit www.skinnywhitechick.com.

The Writers

Those who create worlds with their words are indeed mages within the Faery community. There are many incredible writers working within the fantasy genre, in many different styles. I was able to interview three outstanding individuals—one that is famous within his field and two wonderful new writers—all with wonderful insights to share.

Charles de Lint

Charles de Lint is an internationally renowned, award-winning fantasy author of over thirty novels, many of which, such as *Moonheart* and *Widdershins*, bring the world of Faery into direct contact with the modern urban environment. He is an active member of the Faery community, appearing at many events in the United States. He is also a talented folk musician and has recently released his first album, *Old Blue Truck*. He was good enough to take the time to answer a few of my questions about his perceptions of Faery and the inspirations behind his work.

Your readers love the way you bring traditional folktales and mythic themes into a contemporary setting. Why do you think Faery is relevant to the modern world?

If by Faery you mean an otherness, a sense that we share the world with beings and things and places that we can't always see, I believe it opens up possibilities. When the wear and tear of the world we normally experience bears down on us—the rush, the noise, the traffic, possibly the less-than-satisfying job—it's comforting to imagine that there is more than what we can easily see. That there's a place that respects the bond between beings and their environment, and celebrates the idea of everything being connected. And even in the darker aspects of Faery there are lessons to be learned, guideposts that we can take with us and use to better ourselves and the "real" world in which we spend so much of our time.

Having just come back from playing at a Faerie festival called FaerieWorlds in Eugene, Oregon, I can also add that Faerie also appears to be a place where one can find joy and an openness one doesn't usually find in the world at large. There seems to be little pretence in the costuming; rather, it's a celebration and an artistic expression that infuses both those dressing up and those who don't. It reminded me a little of hippie music festivals in the sixties, and I'm delighted to see an upsurge in simpler values that include embracing the people around you.

Book cover images used
courtesy of Tor Books

What are your main influences as a writer?

Creativity gains its inspiration from everything we experience, it doesn't matter one's particular medium (and I've noticed that most creative people express themselves in more than one). I think of art as one big conversation, with the huge benefit of allowing us to enter a discourse with the great artists of the past as well as our contemporaries. Ideas for stories come to me from a song I might hear, a story I read, a film, a dance. I don't mean that I borrow the idea from the original source—rather, I have something to add to the ongoing conversation.

Does your writing reflect your own spiritual beliefs or is it purely fantasy?

It depends what aspect you're referring to. Unlike, say, Brian Froud, I haven't had the good fortune of actually seeing fairies, but I certainly sense and seek out the mysteries in the world. I believe that everything has a spirit, everything is connected, and that mystery and wonder should always be celebrated.

You are also a folk singer. Why are the old tales and songs important to you?

The traditional music—especially instrumental tunes—seems to speak directly to the heart at the same time as it moves the body. I love that about it, and it's what drew me to playing jigs and reels and slow airs in the first place. I also love how you can get together musicians from Canada, Ireland, the States, and Australia, and they can all find something to play because the tunes travel pretty much unchanged throughout the world. As for the ballads and songs, they're narratives, and they appeal to me for the same reason that folktales and fairy tales do. They awake my sense of wonder, and I love the poetic turn of phrase sitting side by side with a very down-to-earth line.

Although I've played the old traditional music for years, over the past decade or so I've turned more to contemporary story songs. I suppose it's because the narratives take place in more familiar settings, much the way the settings in the old ballads were familiar to the listeners at the time that those songs were first composed.

I've just put out my first album, *Old Blue Truck*, after thirty years of meaning to do so, and I'm delighted by the response from listeners. The songs seem to appeal to them in the same way that music appeals to me, and that's a most gratifying thing.

. . . .

For more information, visit www.charlesdelint.com.

Karen Mahoney

Karen Mahoney is a talented, young, up-and-coming writer of fantasy fiction for young adults who lives in London, UK. She is the author of the Iron Witch trilogy of books in which Faery plays a crucial part. Karen was good enough to take the time to answer a few questions and give some insight into her inspirations and creative process.

What or who inspired you to start writing, and why Faery?

I always wanted to write. I'm one of those writers—you know, the ones who want to write as soon as they can pick up a pen and make marks on a page. Maybe even before then! So I can't really say who inspired me to write, because it honestly feels like it all came with the package when I first arrived in this world.

The *what* is a little easier—stories. Stories inspired me to write and to tell my own, because I loved them so much from such a young age. One of my favourite kinds of story when I was a kid, and still today as an adult, were fairy tales. I'm pretty passionate about folklore, and that's when I first met the many denizens of Faery. To me, all the different lore and mythology around faeries talk about magic and possibility and transformation and hope and danger and adventure—all of that wonderful stuff.

Have you had any real-life experiences with Faery?

I once took part in a Faery workshop. The woman running it was encouraging us to interact with the Faery realm and, to be honest, when I first participated I was a bit cynical. Yeah, I love the stories, but that's all there was to it...right? That's what I thought. Then I did this workshop (sort of as research), and I had an experience during a visualization where I was lost in a sprawling wood. My only way out was to follow a path that kept disappearing beneath my feet. So my only way to find the path was to follow footprints that couldn't possibly have been made by anything human.

Now, I was fully awake when we were doing this group exercise, but my imagination took off, and years later, when I sat down to write *The Iron Witch*, those footprints came back to haunt me and became the basis for the Wood Monster in my book. That's a Faery creature who haunts the Ironwood and is controlled by the Wood Queen (the queen of the dark elves). I have to admit, that workshop visualization felt pretty real...

What do you perceive the nature of Faery to be?

For me, Faery encapsulates all stories and folklore—the tales that form us as we grow from children to adults. Those stories, and the people and magical creatures that fill them, act as signposts to help us along the way in our journey. If you read books like *Women Who Run with the Wolves* by Dr. Clarissa Pinkola Estés, you can see how powerful folklore is—how it shapes us as human beings. Faery is a big part of that.

Do you believe you have a muse?

I don't think I have a muse in the traditional sense, but there is one piece of folklore that I feel leads me and inspires my work: "The Handless Maiden." It's not such a well-known tale as others, but it's incredibly potent and speaks of a girl's journey to adulthood—the transformation into a woman. *The Iron Witch* was definitely inspired by that particular piece of lore, and I think "The Handless Maiden" will be a part of my creative journey for a long time to come. Perhaps that can be considered a muse of sorts.

What is the aim of your work, and what direction
would you like it to take in the future?

My work is currently mainly for young adults, and my number one aim is to entertain and inspire readers with the magic and possibility of stories. I have a variety of faerie characters in The Iron Witch trilogy, from the manipulative Wood Queen (leader of the dark elves) to the half-faerie Xan, whom my main character, Donna Underwood, falls for. In the future, I can see including many other types of faerie characters and exploring more of the Faery realm in my work, but there's just so much folklore and mythology that speaks to me, I wouldn't want to limit myself! I think as long as my writing keeps feeling exciting to me, then it will hopefully feel that way to others. I specifically like to write strong female characters, and I believe that's especially important when you're writing for teenagers.

For more information, visit www.kazmahoney.com.

Cliff Seruntine

Cliff Seruntine is a mystic, psychologist, and woodsman living in the wilds of Nova Scotia, Canada. His first novel, *An Ogham Wood*, was released in 2011, and he has a number of other titles in the works. He has also written a book about Celtic Druidic traditions, *The Lore of the Bard* (Llewellyn, 2003), under the pseudonym Arthur Rowan. He is an inspiring figure to anyone who wishes to truly live in harmony with nature, and his very real connection the realm of Faery and nature spirits is evident in his work. He shares some of his inspiration with us here.

How can fantasy writing increase understanding of the truth of Faery?

Fantasy written with knowledge and art can not only shed light on the lore of Faerie but also help the reader develop a broader perspective. Ideally it will help the reader perceive as faerie denizens might. This is important because, let's face it, most of the old myths and folklore (while beautiful and intriguing) portray the Faerie realm from an entirely anthropocentric perspective. Think about it: how many fairy tales have you read where Jack's goal was to rob from the faeries, yet he is portrayed as the good guy? Jack sneaks into faerie lands and faerie households and steals treasures of gold, marvellous magical artefacts, perhaps even a lovely faerie damsel. But then the faeries are portrayed as cruel and hostile when they hunt Jack down and take back what's theirs. In fact, when you think about it, it's really the humans that are the bad guys in many of the folktales, constantly looking for opportunities to take advantage of faerie beings. Good fantasy, I think, will help readers perceive things more fairly and in more depth.

When I wrote *An Ogham Wood*, I wanted very much to put myself in the mind of the faerie folk. I asked myself what would beings that have done no harm and been in retreat from us for eons think of us. How would they perceive the changes we have wrought upon the world? Would they understand such distinctly human acts as romance and war? How would they relate, being creatures of nature, to human drives for shelter, community, and order? How would they, being not human, make sense of human emotions? They are not humans and must perceive the world in ways that defy our concepts. I tried to take my mind as much out of human thinking as possible. I think I was able to do this because I have lived so much of my life in wild places. For me, relating to animals and nature was often not just an abstract goal, it was a matter of survival. I took what I learned of the minds of wild creatures and the fickle, loving, yet indifferent moods of nature itself, and applied that to the faerie mind. And from that I created the faerie characters that inhabit the Ogham Wood. And I found it was much like what a shaman does when the shaman enters a spirit mind or allows a spirit to enter his mind.

And in this, I think, is the value of fantasy writing—entering and relating a fey perspective. Such writing broadens the mind, helps writer and reader see through spirit eyes, comprehend through fey wisdom.

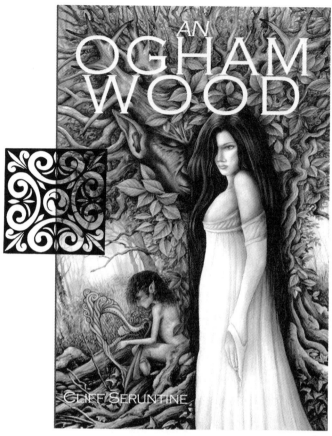

Cover image by Marc Potts, courtesy of Avalonia Books
(www.avaloniabooks.co.uk)

Why is Faery important to you?

Since I was a child, I have perceived two human worlds. There is the one we are building for ourselves now. It is a world of fascinating trinkets and endless theories of how everything works. It seems to offer a lot of promise in that it holds answers and can amuse us endlessly. I mean, nowadays we have talking cars that can tell you how to navigate anywhere on the planet, cell phones that let you watch videos and access email, the capacity to communicate by video or text to anyone anywhere. But it is a world that answers a lot of hows and very little in the way of whys. And its veneer of trinkets and amusement come at a high price. It pollutes the land, the sea, and sky everywhere. And it separates us from the things that are at the foundation of our being: the land which gives us food. The sea which gives us water and air. This world is ephemeral, recently come and unsustainable, devoid of spirit, soon to vanish.

The other world I see is much simpler and older and more durable. Our elders have been in touch with it since the mythic age, and we can be too. It is a world rich with nature and life on levels from the microbes in the soil to the spirits in the trees. It is a world enriched by ancient story, and it is beautifully haunted by myriad spirits. This is sustainable world, closer to the natural realm of Faerie. And to know it, we need only live close to that which is alive and good for us, allow ourselves a bit of imagination and a bit of deeper sight. To me, it is the more valuable world. It is fair and fey, full of wondrous mystery, and it is where true wisdom and depth lie.

What change do you hope to bring into the world through your life and work?

Anyone who knows me knows I live a simple life immersed in nature. I live on a homestead deep in the woods. I grow a lot of my own food. I train horses and track wildlife. I make it a daily practice to commune with nature and also frequently enter the forests for no other reason than to talk with the trees and the beings that reside among them. I hope to inspire people to live lives that are closer to the land, closer to things that have true value. I am a strong believer that if one has food and shelter, if one has family and friends, therein is the greatest treasure. I think persons who realize these things come very close to experiencing the true mystery of Faerie, that wildly incomprehensible, beautifully magical place, for themselves. In my writing, I hope to share that in a way that touches not only the intellect but the heart, for in the end it is our hearts —our dreams and passions—that drive us to create the world we live in.

For more information, visit cliffseruntine.wordpress.com.

"The other world I see is much simpler
and older and more durable. Our
elders have been in touch with it since
the mythic age, and we can be too. It
is a world rich with nature and life
on levels from the microbes in the
soil to the spirits in the trees. It is a
world enriched by ancient story, and
it is beautifully haunted by myriad
spirits. This is sustainable world,
closer to the natural realm of Faerie."

Cliff Seruntine

• • • • • • •

Suggested Activities

Give Thanks

Think about those who inspire you most, particularly those who inspire you to delve further into the realm of Faery. Choose one (or more, if you wish) in particular and make contact with them if you can, writing a letter thanking them for the inspiration. This will encourage them to carry on their good work and inspire others!

Inspire Others

How can you inspire others to connect with the realm of Faery? What are your strengths? Perhaps you simply lead by example, or perhaps you could do something more consciously. Consider writing a blog of your experiences working through this book and your ongoing path into Faery.

Create

It might be interesting to trace your sources of inspiration. In this information age, it is easy to do research on the background of those who have inspired you. Draw out a family tree of inspiration with yourself in the roots, moving up to your main sources of inspiration, those who inspired them further up in the branches, and so on; see how far you can get! Equally consider those whom you may have inspired, and place them as your offshoots. Who will they go on to inspire in return?

If you are pleased with the result, you could frame it and place it in your home as a reminder of your part in the flow of inspiration.

CHAPTER EIGHT
Balance

"B-A-L-A-N-C-E...*Balance!*"

Juan Sánchez Villa-Lobos Ramírez, *Highlander*

• • • • • • •

Through the chapters of this book we have looked at the qualities of the seven points of the Faery Craft septagram: knowledge, connection, trust, honour, magick, joy, and inspiration. However, there is an eighth point, and that is the centre of the star. From the core we learn to keep all the above in balance in our lives, which all interrelate and complement each other.

The Core of the Septagram

We inform ourselves with knowledge, using our discernment to judge what is relevant to our path and what increases our understanding of others and the world around us. Just as air feeds fire, knowledge feeds our inspiration and empowers our magick. When, through acquiring the proper knowledge of how to do so, we honour our otherworldly allies, we build strong connections with them and the world around us. Through this connection we build trust between us, and within trust may be found great joy.

From the central point of balance, which can only be found through a proper exploration and understanding of the seven points above, the path ahead becomes clear, and we

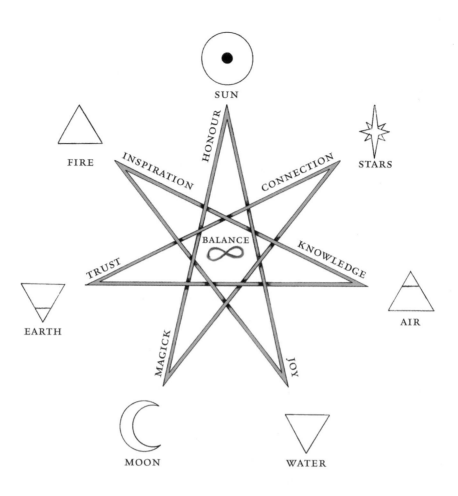

SUN

HONOUR

FIRE

INSPIRATION

CONNECTION

STARS

BALANCE
∞

TRUST

KNOWLEDGE

EARTH

MAGICK

JOY

AIR

MOON

WATER

Faery Craft septagram
by Tamara Newman
(www.tamaranewman.com)

may walk forward with our Faery allies in honour and joy, with trust in our connection, sharing the inspiration of our magick with the world, so that more and more may have the knowledge of the truth of Faery Craft.

EXERCISE: *Walking the Septagram*

Note that if walking outdoors is difficult, this may also be performed internally as a visualisation.

Find a large, even patch of ground outdoors where you can walk without fear of tripping or of being disturbed. Perform the Becoming the Faery Tree exercise on page 50 to ground yourself and connect with your surroundings. Breathe deeply and evenly, and calm your mind.

You are standing at the top point of the septagram, in the position of the sun and the direction of within. Feel the power of your inner light radiating from your centre. There is a sun above you, and there is a sun within you, your own divine light. This is where you carry your honour, which accompanies you always through your Faery Craft. Consider how the quality of honour manifests in your life and all you have learnt in the pages and exercises of this book. Take three deep breaths, breathing in the quality of honour and breathing out any dishonour that has been done to or by you during your life. Keeping the light of the sun and honour with you in your centre, move forward and to the right seven paces to the next point of the septagram, the moon. Turn to face the direction from whence you came.

The moon represents the below, what dwells beneath the surface both in the world around us and within us, and represents the quality of magick. Here is the sublunar realm and the source of Faery magick. Feel the power of the moon in your pelvic area. Take three deep breaths and consider the power of magick at work in your life and all you have learnt in the pages and exercises of this book. Breathe in the quality of magick and breathe out any memories of disenchantment in your life or the world around you. Carrying both honour and magick with you, step forward and to the right seven paces to the next point of the septagram, the stars. Turn to face the direction from whence you came.

The stars represent the quality of connection and the direction of above. Feel the power of the stars within your forehead and know that you are intrinsically connected not only to the world around you but to the cosmos. Take three deep breaths and consider the quality of connection at work within your life and all you have learnt in the pages and exercises of this book. Breathe in the quality of connection and breathe out any times of disconnection within yourself and the world. Carrying honour, magick, and connection with you, step forward and to the right seven paces a third time, to find yourself at the next point of the septagram, earth. Turn to face the direction from whence you came.

Earth comes from the direction of north and the quality of trust. Feel the power of earth within your flesh and bones. Consider your relationship with your Faery allies and all you have learnt in the pages of this book. Take three deep breaths, breathing in the quality of trust and breathing out any thoughts or memories of distrust and betrayal. Taking all the qualities this far with you, walk forward and to the right seven paces again, taking you to the next point of the septagram, air. Turn to face the direction from whence you came.

Air comes from the direction of east and the quality of knowledge. Feel the power of air within your breath. Consider your relationship with the quality of knowledge and all you have learnt in the pages of this book. Take three deep breaths, breathing in the quality of knowledge and breathing out any ignorance and misunderstanding of the past. Holding all the qualities so far within you, move forward and to the right seven paces again, to reach the next point of the septagram, fire. Turn to face the direction from whence you came.

Fire comes from the direction of south and is associated with the quality of inspiration. Feel the power of fire within the heat of your body and the electric signals that are constantly at work within you. Consider how you act upon inspiration in your life and what has inspired you within the pages of this book. How will you act upon this inspiration? Take three deep breaths, breathing in the quality of inspiration and breathing out any times of inaction or creative blockage. Holding awareness of all the qualities thus far within you, step forward and to the right seven paces to the last point of the septagram, water. Turn to face the centre of the septagram.

Water comes from the direction of west and represents the quality of joy. Feel the power of water within your body, within your riverlike veins, your blood, tears, sweat, and hormones. Consider the presence of joy in your life and what has brought you joy within the pages of this book. Take three deep breaths, breathing in the quality of joy and breathing out despair and boredom.

Now, holding all the qualities of honour, magick, connection, earth, air, fire, and water with you, step forward into the centre of the septagram. Feel all the qualities at work within your life and the world around you in balance. Take three deep breaths, breathing in the quality of balance and breathing out any imbalance or unwanted chaos.

Whilst in the centre, perform the Becoming the Faery Tree exercise once more to ground yourself, then reflect on your experience, walking back into everyday life with all the qualities of Faery Craft in balance within you.

The Raven King's Daughter

Once upon a time, be it long ago, this very moment, or perhaps in years to come, the Faery Court of the West was ruled by the wise and ancient Raven King. The Court of the East was ruled by the White Queen, who often walked the land in the form of a great white mare.

But twice a year, when the day and night were of equal length, the king and queen would meet at the boundary between their two lands, at the blessed mound of Silbury Hill. And there, while their clans celebrated in the halls beneath, the Raven King and the White Queen would meet in private at the top of the hill by silvery moon and discuss the fate of mankind.

The wisdom of the Raven King had kept the peace for many ages, but in the days we speak of, his patience was growing thin. No longer did it seem so wise to let the ills of man and their greedy deeds go unchecked, and yet the White Queen sang to him always of peace.

319

She loved the passion with which he raved, and he loved the beauty of her peaceful song, and between them, on a spring night, they made a daughter of true royal Faery blood, with the passion of her father and the beauty of her mother.

When the Raven King's daughter had almost reached her bloom, she heard the ravings of her father and knew that his heart was at last determined upon war.

Placing her hand upon his heart, she pleaded with him to keep the peace.

"Father," she urged, "to be sure, must we not know the truth of their hearts? Let me go amongst them and see whether I may learn it, for surely war is a dreadful thing!"

The king examined his daughter's face.

"Are you so determined, my precious child? For you know that to fully enter the world of mortals, you must die to us and be reborn to them, and this you may do only four times, as the paths of the crossroads allow, before you return to us at last..."

"Father, I am determined," she replied, "and willing to make this sacrifice for lasting peace."

The Raven King could see the truth in his daughter's eyes, and he knew there would be no dissuading her. And so it was that the Raven King devoured his daughter and went to the crossroads where the worlds meet.

There, alongside the first path, he saw a silver fish swimming in the river, so he visited himself upon the fish, and the Raven King's daughter was born into the world of man as a fish.

Her life as a fish was short, for as she swam to get near the first men she saw, she was caught in their nets and sold to market.

When her spirit returned to the land of Faery, her father asked, "Tell me, what have you learnt of the heart of man?"

The Raven King's daughter replied, "Father, I have learnt of their greed, but I think I saw a tinge of regret in the eyes of the man who caught me. Please, Father, I must return again!"

So the Raven King devoured his daughter and returned to the crossroads where the worlds meet. There on the second path he saw a bird sitting high in the branches of a tree, so he visited himself upon it, and the Raven king's daughter was born into the world as a bird. Her life as a bird was long, for she flew high above the world of man, who seemed barely to notice her at all, yet she saw all their quarrels and the devastating effects of their growth and destruction.

When her spirit returned to the land of Faery, her father asked again, "Tell me, what have you learnt of the heart of man?"

"Father," she replied, "I have learnt of their short-sightedness—and yet I saw some invention and ingenuity in the world they are creating for themselves. Please, Father, I must return again."

So the Raven King devoured his daughter and went to the crossroads where the worlds meet. There on the third path was waiting a sturdy Shire horse, and he visited himself upon it. So his daughter was born once more into the world, this time as a horse.

Her life as a horse was long and hard, carrying luggage and heavy travellers over great distances.

When she returned to the land of Faery, her father asked, "Tell me, what have you learned of the heart of man?"

"Father, I have learned of their selfishness, yet the songs and stories they tell each other on their long journeys fill my heart with hope. Let me return once more?"

"This must be your final birth, daughter, for when you have at last returned again to the land of Faery, the paths of the crossroads may not be walked again into the land of mortals…"

And so the Raven King devoured his daughter for a final time and went to the cross-roads where the worlds meet. There on the fourth path was a beautiful yet wretched woman who seemed to have been waiting there for days. The Raven King looked into her mind and took the form of the one for whom she was waiting, and so it was that the Raven king's daughter came into the world of man as a woman at last.

After a childhood full of discovery and tragedy, her heart was worn and heavy, and yet at last she met one who seemed happy to carry its weight for her. He was simple and true, and she knew she had found what she had been looking for.

He even went with her as far as the crossroads, but she did not pass into the land of Faery, for her heart now belonged to a mortal man. He, in turn, had given his heart to her, and she was able to see at last the truth that lay within. She left her farewells at the crossroads and remained for the rest of her mortal life in the world of man, where she married and had many children. Her children grew in their turn and had children of their own, and so on it went...

So that is why the Raven King will not go to war with the world of man, for his daughter and her children, his descendants, live here still. In each of their hearts there lies a seed of Faery that is still seeking for the truth of men's hearts, will ever seek out the best in those they meet, and will ever sing their song to the green wood and the hollow hills...

Emily Carding, 2010

• • • • • •

Acknowledgments

The first share must always go to them, the spirits of rock, tree, and river, who inspired many of the exercises and musings of this book. Unending thanks also to my husband, Jules (aka Bear), for amazing support, and daughter, Willow, for putting up with my grumpy author persona.

Huge thanks to Barbara Moore for suggesting me for this project, and to Elysia Gallo for her hard work and patience with constant questions.

Thanks to Sorita D'Este for always being so supportive of my work and for so many distracting late-night Skype chats! Big thanks to David Rankine for all the yummy grimoire info and various intriguing leads.

Thanks to R. J. Stewart, John and Caitlín Matthews, the Silver Elves, T. Thorn Coyle, Brian and Wendy Froud, Ari Berk, Elizabeth-Jane Baldry, Charles de Lint, S. J. Tucker, Karen Kay, Felicity Fyr Le Fay, the Dolmen, Linda Ravenscroft, Karen Mahoney, Cliff Seruntine, Lisa Allen, Marc Potts, and Kelly Martinez for taking the time to answer my questions, and to everyone who posed for photos. A big shout-out to Studio Lotus for the great elemental photo shoot done in a day! Thank you also to all the wonderful artists who contributed artwork. I must particularly mention Tamara Newman for creating the Faery Craft septagram whilst recovering from an operation.

Thanks must also go, of course, to the publisher for making this book possible, and to you for reading it now. Faery blessings to you all!

Bibliography

AE. *The Candle of Vision*. London: Macmillan, 1918.

Anderson, Cora. *Fifty Years in the Feri Tradition*. Portland, OR: Harpy Books, 2010.

Barrie, J. M. *Peter Pan and Wendy*. New York: Scribner's, 1921.

Briggs, Katharine. A *Dictionary of Fairies*. Middlesex, UK: Penguin Books, 1976.

———. *The Fairies in Tradition and Literature*. London: Routledge & Kegan Paul, 1967.

Canard, John. *Defenses Against the Witches' Craft*. London: Avalonia Books, 2008.

Carding, Emily. *The Tarot of the Sidhe*. Atglen, PA: Schiffer Books, 2011.

———. *Transparent Tarot*. Atglen, PA: Schiffer Books, 2008.

———. *The Transparent Oracle*. Atglen, PA: Schiffer Books, 2010.

The Chaldean Oracles. By the editors of the Shrine of Wisdom. Surrey, UK: The Shrine of Wisdom, 1979.

D'Este, Sorita (ed). *Both Sides of Heaven*. London: Avalonia Books, 2009.

———. *Hekate: Her Sacred Fires*. London: Avalonia Books, 2010.

———. *Horns of Power*. London: Avalonia Books, 2008.

D'Este, Sorita, and David Rankine. *Practical Planetary Magick*. London: Avalonia Books, 2007.

———. *The Cosmic Shekinah*. London: Avalonia Books, 2011.

———. *The Guises of the Morrigan*. London: Avalonia Books, 2005.

———. *The Isles of the Many Gods*. London: Avalonia Books, 2007.

———. *Visions of The Cailleach*. London: Avalonia Books, 2009.

Digitalis, Raven. *Goth Craft*. Woodbury, MN: Llewellyn Publications, 2007.

Evans-Wentz, W. Y. *The Fairy-Faith in Celtic Countries*. West Valley City, UT: Waking Lion Press, 2006.

Gaiman, Neil, and Charles Vess. *Instructions*. London: Bloomsbury, 2010.

Goswami, Amit. *The Self-Aware Universe*. New York: Putnam's Sons, 1993.

Gregory, Lady Augusta. *Visions and Beliefs in the West of Ireland*. Forgotten Books (http://www.forgottenbooks.org), 1920, 2007.

Hemenway, Priya. *The Secret Code*. Lugano, Switzerland: Evergreen, 2008.

Hole, Christina. *English Folklore*. London: B. T. Batsford Ltd., 1940.

Howard, Michael. *The Book of Fallen Angels*. Somerset, UK: Capall Bann Publishing, 2004.

Hunt, Robert. *Popular Romances of the West of England*. Forgotten Books (http://www.forgottenbooks.org), 1903, 2008.

Johnston, Sarah Iles. *Hekate Soteira*. Atlanta, GA: Scholars Press, 1990.

Kipling, Rudyard. *Puck of Pook's Hill*. New York: Wildside Press, 2008.

Kirk, Robert. *The Secret Commonwealth of Elves, Fauns, and Fairies*. Mineola, NY: Dover Publications, Inc., 2008.

Macleod, Fiona. *At the Turn of the Year, Essays and Nature Thoughts*. Edinburgh, UK: Turnbull and Spears, 1913.

Matthews, John, and Caitlín Matthews. *The Element Encyclopedia of Magical Creatures*. London: HarperElement, 2005.

———. *The Encyclopaedia of Celtic Myth and Legend*. London: BCA, 2002.

Matthews, John. *The Sidhe: Wisdom from the Celtic Otherworld*. Issaquah, WA: The Lorian Association, 2004.

Norton, Rosaleen. *Thorn in the Flesh*. York Beach, ME: Teitan Press, 2009.

Pollington, Stephen. *Leechcraft*. Ely, Cambs., UK: Anglo-Saxon Books, 2008.

Rankine, David. *Crystals Healing and Folklore*. Somerset, UK: Capall Bann Publishing, 2002.

———. *The Book of Treasure Spirits*. London: Avalonia Books, 2009.

Seymour-Smith, Martin. *The New Astrologer*. London: Sidgwick and Jackson, 1981.

Spence, Lewis. *The Magic Arts in Celtic Britain*. London: Rider & Co., 1945.

Stewart, R. J. *The Living World of Faery*. Lake Toxaway, NC: Mercury Publishing, 1995.

Yeats, W. B. "The Stolen Child" in *The Wanderings of Oisin, and Other Poems*. London: Paul, Trench & Co., 1889.

Index

To Write to the Author

If you wish to contact the author or would like more information about this book, please write to the author in care of Llewellyn Worldwide and we will forward your request. Both the author and the publisher appreciate hearing from you and learning of your enjoyment of this book and how it has helped you. Llewellyn Worldwide cannot guarantee that every letter written to the author can be answered, but all will be forwarded. Please write to:

Emily Carding
℅ Llewellyn Worldwide
2143 Wooddale Drive
Woodbury, MN 55125-2989
Please enclose a self-addressed stamped envelope for reply,
or $1.00 to cover costs. If outside the U.S.A., enclose an
international postal reply coupon.

Many of Llewellyn's authors have websites with additional information and resources. For more information, please visit our website:

WWW.LLEWELLYN.COM